QUESTIONS AND ANSWERS

FOR

MOTOR VEHICLE MECHANICS

New Series

by

ROY BROOKS

A. M. I. M. I.

Senior Lecturer in Motor Vehicle Subjects
Bolton College of Education (Technical)

Drake Publishers Inc.
New York

CONTENTS

FIRST YEAR
MOTOR VEHICLE TECHNOLOGY

SECOND YEAR

MOTOR VEHICLE TECHNOLOGY

THIRD YEAR
MOTOR VEHICLE TECHNOLOGY

FOURTH YEAR

MOTOR VEHICLE TECHNOLOGY

CONTENTS

Calculations, Science and Laboratory Work

Electrical

QUESTIONS AND ANSWERS

FOR

MOTOR VEHICLE MECHANICS

New Series

FIRST YEAR

MOTOR VEHICLE TECHNOLOGY

SAFETY PRECAUTIONS
AND GENERAL WORKSHOP
REGULATIONS

1. List five common sense safety precautions that should be applied in garage work.

(a) Never run in the workshop. (b) Always be certain that a vehicle is in neutral before starting the engine. (c) Do not work under a vehicle supported solely by a jack. (d) Always use unworn, good-fitting wrenches. (e) Be sure you know the position of the fire extinguishers in the workshop and how to use them.

2. Why is it particularly dangerous to smoke or use a naked light in an inspection pit?

Because inflammable gasoline fumes, being heavier than air, tends to collect in such places and thus the fire risk there will be greater.

3. How is it possible to determine the maximum load that say a crane, jack, or set of lifting blocks is intended to take?

The 'Safe Working Load' (S.W.L.) should be found painted, stamped, or in some other way marked on the equipment. This load should never be exceeded.

4. What two most important regulations must be observed when putting gasoline into a vehicle's fuel tank?

(a) The engine must be stopped. (b) No smoking.

5. Why is it important not to wear loose-fitting or ragged overalls in a workshop?

To minimize the risk of such clothing being caught up in machinery (e.g. a drill) which could lead to personal injury.

13

CONVENTIONAL CAR LAYOUT
AND FUNCTION OF MAIN COMPONENTS

6. Place the following list of components in the correct order of power transmission from the engine to the drive wheels: Engine, drive wheels, clutch, master and pinion, transmission, axle drive shafts, propeller shaft.

Engine, clutch, transmission, propeller shaft, master and pinion wheel, axle drive shafts, drive wheels.

7. What are three reasons for the use of a clutch?

(a) To enable the vehicle to move away smoothly from rest. *(b)* To assist in gear-changing. *(c)* To provide a temporary position of neutral.

8. What is the purpose of a transmission?

(a) To enable the torque (twisting force) being transmitted from the engine to the driving wheels to be varied in accordance with load and speed requirements. *(b)* To provide a means of reversing the vehicle. *(c)* To provide a permanent position of neutral.

9. With a car of conventional layout, why is the rear axle called a 'live axle'?

Because it houses the master and pinion (final drive) and differential assembly, and the axle drive shafts (driving shafts) which drive the driving wheels.

10. What is a 'motor vehicle chassis'?

A chassis comprises everything except the body, cab, and equipment. (It is not just the chassis frame.)

11. Some vehicles do not employ a separate chassis frame. Give three different names by which this type of construction is known.

(a) Chassisless construction. *(b)* Integral construction. *(c)* Monocoque construction.

12. What is the function of the engine?

To convert (by combustion, i.e. burning) the heat energy contained in the gasoline into mechanical energy to provide the motive power for the vehicle and drive the various accessories such as generator and alternator and water-pump.

HAND TOOLS AND LAYOUT

13. Name three types of wrenches and give an example of their use.

(a) Open-end wrench, used for general purpose work and particularly where the wrench can only be fitted on to the nut from the side
(and not from above or below). *(b)* Box wrench, useful where space
around a nut is limited and where wrench movement is restricted.
(c) Socket wrench, used in conjunction with extensions, ratchet or
speed-handle, etc., can be particularly useful in speeding up nut and
bolt removal and replacement, and also working on nuts and bolts
in inaccessible positions.

**14. List three common hand-tools used for cutting or removing
metal and give an example of their use.**

(a) Hacksaw, for sawing through such things as metal bars and
tubes. *(b)* File, for trimming to final shape and smoothing off metal
objects. *(c)* Cold chisel, for relatively rough work such as speedily
removing rusted nuts.

**15. How can easily marked objects, such as a chromium-plated
door handle or a brass casting, be safely held in a vice?**

By means of detachable 'jaw guards,' made of soft material such
as fibre or aluminum positioned ,so as to cover the serrated steel
faces of the vice jaws.

16. How are wrench sizes marked?

Wrenches are marked according to the distance across the 'flats'
of the bolt head or nut. The diameter of the bolt plus 3/16" will
give the wrench size. Thus a 1/4 bolt takes a 7/16 wrench, a 5/16
bolt takes a 1/2 wrench, etc.

**17. List four bench tools which may be sharpened on a bench
grinder.**

(a) Cold chisel. *(b)* Scriber. *(c)* Center punch. *(d)* Twist drill.

**18. Suggest five common sense rules that should be observed
when sharpening tools on a bench grinder.**

(a) Goggles must be worn. *(b)* Tool-rest should be adjusted to
within about 1/16" of the grinding wheel. *(c)* Hold the object to be
ground firmly, but do not jab it fiercely on to the wheel. *(d)* Keep
the tip of the tool cool by frequently dipping it into water. *(e)* Never
use a wheel that has a badly chipped grinding face.

19. **List three tools commonly used in 'marking out' metal.**
(a) Scriber. *(b)* Dividers. *(c)* Steel try-square.

20. **How is it possible to make layout lines easily visible on, say, a steel block.**
By cleaning the face to be laid out and then smearing it lightly with Prussian blue or copper sulphate solution. Any marks then made on it will score through and show up brightly in contrast.

ENGINES

21. **Name in order the four strokes of the Otto, or four-stroke, cycle.**
Intake. Compression. Power. Exhaust.

22. **Describe briefly what happens on each of the four strokes.**
Intake: Piston descends, drawing a mixture of gasoline vapor and air into the cylinder through the open intake valve.
Compression: Both valves are closed. Piston rises and compresses the mixture.
Power: Just before the end of the compression stroke the spark ignites the mixture, which then burns very rapidly, causing a high increase in pressure within the cylinder. This forces the piston downward on its 'working' stroke. Both valves are still closed.
Exhaust: Piston rises and expels the burnt gases through the open exhaust valve.

23. **Each of the following diagrams represents one stroke of the Otto cycle. Name each stroke shown.**

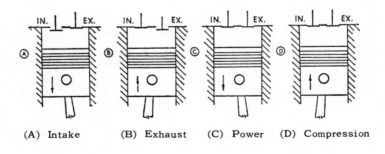

(A) Intake   (B) Exhaust   (C) Power   (D) Compression

24. How many engine revolutions are required to complete the four-stroke cycle?

Two revolutions.

25. Name the lettered parts of the engine (shown in unit with its clutch and transmission). *See Fig. p. 18.*

(A) Air-filter and silencer. (B) Oil filler-cap and breather. (C) Piston. (D) Distributor. (E) Oil pump. (F) Oil filter. (G) Oil pan. (H) Camshaft. (I) Starter motor. (J) Crankshaft. (K) Connecting rod. (L) Transmission. (M) Clutch. (N) Valve. (O) Flywheel.

26. Multi-cylinder engines are used in preference to single-cylinder engines which would give the same output. Compare a large single-cylinder engine with an engine having four small cylinders to show the reasons for this preference. (Both four-stroke engines.)

Large Single-cylinder Engine:

(*a*) Jerky torque from only one power stroke per two revolutions.

(*b*) Heavy flywheel required.

(*c*) Large piston and valves present considerable cooling difficulties.

(*d*) Large exhaust pulsations are difficult to silence.

(*e*) The engine would be very tall and difficult to accommodate under the hood.

(*f*) Engine would be very heavy.

(*g*) The heavy piston would be difficult to balance.

(*h*) Must be a slow-speed engine.

Engine with Four Small Cylinders:

(*a*) Two power strokes per revolution giving smooth torque output.

(*b*) Lighter flywheel, allowing quicker acceleration.

(*c*) Small valves and pistons are easier to cool.

(*d*) More frequent and smaller exhaust pulsations are easier to silence.

(*e*) Engine is much more compact.

(*f*) This engine would be only about half the weight of the single-cylinder engine.

(*g*) Quite good balance is possible.

(*h*) Could be run at much higher r.p.m.

ENGINE DISMANTLING AND FUNCTION OF PARTS

27. In what general sequence would you dismantle a simple four-cylinder, o.h.v. engine?

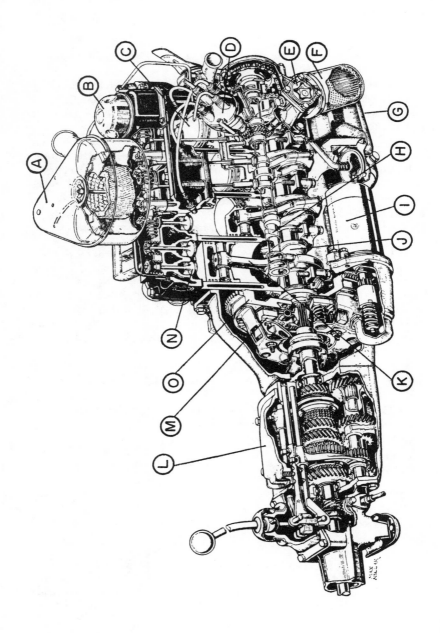

After draining coolant and engine oil remove the following in order: Accessories (e.g. distributor, starter, generator and alternator, etc.). cylinder head, valve gear, oil pan, timing gear cover, timing chain, connecting rod bearing caps and withdraw con-rods and pistons, flywheel, camshaft, main bearing caps, and crank shaft.

28. What is the function of an engine flywheel?

(a) To store up energy to help the engine over its 'idle' strokes. (b) To dampen out speed fluctuations of the crankshaft due to the varying effect of the firing impulses during the engine cycle. (c) It provides a convenient mounting-point for the clutch and starter ring gear.

29. What is the purpose of a connecting rod?

To connect the piston to the crankshaft and change the reciprocating (backward-and-forward) motion of the piston into the rotary motion of the cranksahft.

30. What are the functions of a piston?

(a) It must form a sliding, gas- and oil-tight seal within the cylinder. (b) It must transmit the gas load to the small end of the connecting rod. (c) It generally must act as a bearing for the piston-pin.

31. Why are cylinder heads made detachable?

(a) Decarbonizing and valve-grinding can be more easily carried out. (b) In some cases the pistons must be removed upward. (c) Easier to rebore. (d) In the case of a cracked block or head only the affected part would need to be renewed and not the complete unit.

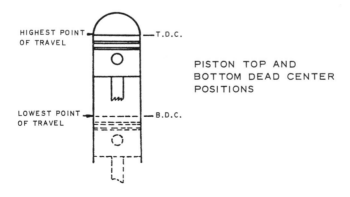

HIGHEST POINT OF TRAVEL — T.D.C.

LOWEST POINT OF TRAVEL — B.D.C.

PISTON TOP AND BOTTOM DEAD CENTER POSITIONS

32. What do the initials 't.d.c.' and 'b.d.c.' stand for?
See Fig. p. 19.

T.d.c. means *top dead center*. This is the highest point reached by the top of the piston in its travel up the cylinder bore. B.d.c. means *bottom dead center*. This is the lowest point in the cylinder bore reached by the top of the piston.

FUEL SUPPLY SYSTEM AND CARBURETOR

33. Name in order, from the tank to the engine, the various parts of a conventional fuel supply system.

Fuel tank, pipe line to pump, fuel pump, pipe line (usually incorporating flexible section) from pump to carburetor, carburetor.

34. Name three different fuel pipe connections or unions.

(*a*) Olive and nut. (*b*) Soldered nipple and nut. (*c*) Push-on neoprene tube.

35. What is the basic function of a carburetor?

To mix gasoline and air in correct proportions and to supply an appropriate quantity of that mixture to meet varying engine requirements.

36. Show, by means of a sketch, how a simple type carburetor works.

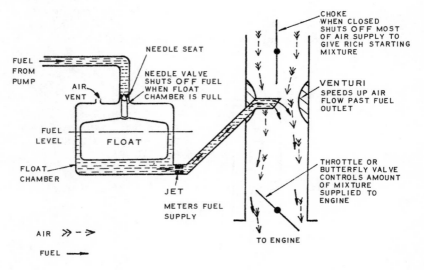

TWO-STROKE ENGINE

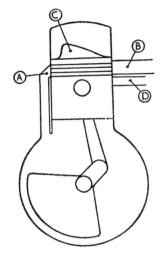

37. What is the name of the working cycle of the engine shown?

The 'two-stroke' cycle.

38. What is the name and function of port A?

This is the 'transfer port,' through which the mixture is transferred from below to above the piston.

39. State the name of port B and explain how it functions.

This is the 'exhaust port.' Downward movement of the piston uncovers this port so that the burnt gases can escape through it.

40. Name the part of the piston labelled C and explain its purpose.

This is the 'deflector.' Its purpose is to deflect the incoming mixture upward, thus reducing mixture loss through the exhaust port and assisting the expulsion of the burnt gases.

41. What is the name and function of port D?

This is the 'intake port,' through which, with the piston in a suitable position, new mixture passes from the carburetor into the crankcase.

42. Describe the sequence of events in a two-stroke engine when the piston is on its downward stroke and ignition has just occurred.

The mixture burns rapidly, causing high cylinder pressures which force the piston downward. About two-thirds of the way down the stroke, the top of the piston uncovers the exhaust port, allowing the exhaust gases to rush out. Shortly afterwards the transfer port is uncovered, and new mixture, which has been lightly compressed by the descending piston, passes from the gas-tight crankcase up the transfer port into the cylinder. This filling of the cylinder continues until the down stroke is completed.

43. Describe the sequence of events occurring as the piston rises in a two-stroke engine.
The rising piston soon closes the transfer and exhaust ports and begins to compress the mixture. As the piston moves upward the effective volume of the crankcase increases, and a partial vacuum is set up. The skirt of the rising piston uncovers the intake port and new mixture is drawn into the crankcase from the carburetor. The charge above the piston is compressed into the combustion space, and just before the end of the upward stroke an electric spark ignites the charge.

44. How many engine revolutions are required to complete the working cycle of a two-stroke engine.
One revolution only.

45. What advantage has a two-stroke gasoline engine over a four-stroke engine?
(a) Fewer moving parts. (b) Cheaper to produce. (c) Smoother torque output with one firing stroke every revolution. (d) Very simple lubrication system.

46. What advantages has a four-stroke engine over a two-stroke engine?
(a) Greater fuel economy. (b) Quieter running. (c) More suitable for large engines. (d) Runs better at lower r.p.m. and generally has a wider range of r.p.m.

47. How is a two-stroke engine normally lubricated?
By the 'total loss' system. Approximately 1/2 pint of oil is mixed with every gallon of gasoline. When the mixture is drawn into the crankcase the gasoline evaporates, leaving some oil clinging to the bearings. Some oil is carried up through the transfer port with the mixture, as oil vapor, to lubricate the cylinder.

48. What are the main causes of misfiring, or 'four-stroking,' of a two-stroke engine at low speeds?

(a) Weak transfer action, so that only a small amount of mixture enters the cylinder. (b) Poor scavenging, particularly of that part of the combustion chamber near the spark plug, so that when the spark occurs it is surrounded by burnt gas, and the new mixture is not ignited.

ENGINE COOLING

49. Some water-cooled engines do not have a water-pump to assist the water circulation. What is the name given to the system then used, and on what principle does it operate?

The thermo-syphon system. This system operates on the principle of natural circulation due to the convection currents formed in liquids when heated. The heated water expands, and becomes less dense. Therefore it rises. As it begins to cool its volume decreases, and so it becomes heavier. Therefore it sinks. As a consequence of these changes, convection currents are set up.

50. List the advantages of thermo-syphon cooling.

(a) Cheap, as no water-pump is required. (b) Reliable, as there are no moving parts. (c) Water action is entirely automatic and depends solely on engine temperature. The hotter the engine, the quicker the circulation.

51. List the disadvantages of thermo-syphon cooling.

(a) In order to achieve efficient circulation the radiator top tank must be well above the engine. This makes for a high hood line. (b) Cool water enters the engine at the bottom of the cylinders, where the engine normally runs fairly cool, and heats up as it rises. When it reaches the top of the cylinders it is hot, and consequently has a reduced cooling effect on the hottest parts of the engine. (c) Difficult to fit an interior heater successfully without a water-pump. (d) Under conditions of very heavy load or in hot climates the water may not circulate as quickly as may be desirable.

52. Why is a pump fitted in the cooling system of most cars?

To ensure more positive water circulation and overcome the disadvantages mentioned in the previous question.

COMMON METALS

53.   What is the difference between cast-iron and mild steel?

Both these metals are (mainly) alloys of iron and carbon. Their main difference lies in the amount of carbon content and its form in the metal. Cast iron is usually thought of as being hard and brittle, whilst mild steel is more malleable (i.e. workable).

54.   Give one example of where each of the following metals may be used, (a) high tensile steel, (b) spring steel, (c) cast iron, (d) mild steel, (e) high carbon sttel, and (f) chrome steel.

(a) Cylinder-head studs, (b) road springs, (c) cylinder blocks, (d) exhaust pipes, (e) twist-drills, (f) exhaust valves.

55.   Suggest several workshop tests that could be used to identify various irons and steels.

Test	Wrought Iron	Cast Iron	Mild Steel	Carbon Steel
Grind	Light stream straw colored sparks	Dull red sparks	Stream of lines and sparks	Heavy stream large sparks
Appearance	Brownish and scaly	Grey	Smooth	Smooth
File	Rough finish	Hard skin crumbling	Cuts easily	Hard. Hardness increasing with carbon content
Drop on ground	Dull sound	Very dull	Slight ring	Higher pitched ring
Hammer when red hot	Flattens easily	Crumbles	Flattens quite easily	Difficult to flatten

TRANSMISSION

56. Make a line diagram to show the transmission layout on a conventional car.

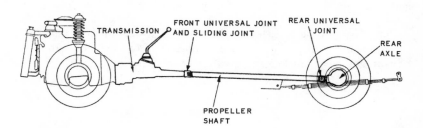

TRANSMISSION FRONT UNIVERSAL JOINT AND SLIDING JOINT REAR UNIVERSAL JOINT REAR AXLE PROPELLER SHAFT

57. What characteristics of an internal combustion engine demand the use of a clutch in order to move the vehicle smoothly away from rest?

The engine must be rotating at several hundred r.p.m. before it can produce sufficient torque (turning power) to be able to move the car away from rest. The clutch is necessary to connect, *in a progressive manner*, the fast revving engine to the stationary transmission, to make possible a smooth take-off from rest.

58. Name the three major parts of a simple single-plate clutch assembly.

Pressure plate, clutch plate (or friction disc), and release bearing.

59. In the simple outline sketch of the three-speed transmission shown below, name the lettered parts.

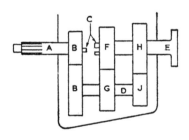

(A) Clutch pilot shaft, alternatively called first motion shaft, spigot shaft, clutch shaft, or stem wheel. (B) Main drive pinion. (C) Synchronizer and clutch unit for top gear. (D) Cluster gear shaft, sometimes called counter shaft. (E) Mainshaft. (F) Second and high sliding gear. (G) Second and high sliding cluster gear shaft. (H) First and reverse sliding gear. (J) First and reverse sliding cluster gear shaft.

60. Why is a low gear normally required to start off from rest?

The torque produced by the engine itself is not sufficient to move the car from rest without stalling. By putting the car into a lower gear, the engine torque is multiplied (at the expense of a lower road speed than would be the case in say top gear, for the same engine r.p.m.).

61. With the engine idling (transmission in neutral, foot off the

clutch), will any of the gears and shafts in the transmission be rotating and if so, which?

Yes, the main drive pinion, cluster gears and the reverse idler gear.

62. What is the general order of dismantling a simple transmission (main parts only)?

Remove in order: the oil, shifter cover, selector mechanism (if separate from the shifter cover), clutch pilot shaft, mainshaft and gears, cluster gear shaft, reverse shaft and idler gear.

Note: In some transmissions it is necessary to remove the cluster gear shaft before the clutch pilot shaft can be removed.

PROPELLER SHAFT AND FINAL DRIVE

63. How many joints has the simple open propeller shaft and what sort are they?

Three, two universal joints, and one sliding joint.

64. What type of bearings are used in 'Hardy-Spicer' type universal joints?

Needle-roller bearings.

65. How are the needle-roller bearings of universal joints normally lubricated?

Generally they are filled with oil during manufacture and require no further lubrication.

66. What is the function of the final drive (master gear and pinion)?

(*a*) To provide a permanent gear reduction. (*b*) To turn the drive through 90° from the propeller shaft to the axle shafts. (*c*) It forms a convenient mounting-point for the differential assembly.

67. Trace the power flow through the various components of a rear axle, from the pinion to the drive wheels. (Assume that the vehicle is travelling under conditions that do not require differential action.)

Pinion, master gear, differential housing, spider pinion shaft, spider pinion gears, axle shaft spider gears also called compensating gears or side gears, axle drive shafts, and drive wheels.

68. Describe the function of the differential.

To allow the two driving wheels to rotate at different speeds (such as when vehicle rounds a bend), yet still receive equal torque.

69. **Answer the following questions relative to the action of a differential, when its master gear is rotating at 500 r.p.m.** *(a)* **If the vehicle was being driven straight on a smooth road and had equal sized wheels at what speed would each axle drive shaft rotate?** *(b)* **If on rounding a bend the inner wheel slowed up by 50 r.p.m., what would be the speed of the outer wheel?**
(a) 500 r.p.m. *(b)* 550 r.p.m.

70. **If the driving wheels of a car were so positioned that one wheel was on a firm surface which gave good traction and the other wheel was on a slippery patch of mud where the tire could get no grip, would the vehicle be able to drive away under these conditions?**
No.

71. **Why could the vehicle in the previous question not be driven away?**
Because of the action of the differential. Although both wheels would be receiving equal torque all the *speed* could go to the wheel with (virtually) no resistance — i.e. the wheel on the mud would spin round, but the other wheel (having no speed) would not move.

72. **What is a rear axle housing vent and why is it necessary?**
A small hole, or vent, to atmosphere. This prevents pressure build-up inside the axle due to temperature increase which occurs during driving. Such a pressure could easily force oil out through oil seals and possibly on to the rear brakes.

SOLDERING

73. **State three important requirements needed to ensure a properly soldered joint.**
(a) Cleanliness. *(b)* Correct soldering temperature. *(c)* Use of correct flux.

74. **Give three examples of where soldering might be employed.**
(a) Soldering a terminal on to a starter lead. *(b)* Soldering a nipple on to a fuel pipe. *(c)* Repairing a leaking radiator joint.

75. **What are the two principal types of soldering fluxes?   Give examples of their use.**

(a) Paste or resin flux, such as may be used on electrical connections. (b) 'Killed acid' flux, which may be used for soldering a patch on an oil drum.

76. What type of flux should be used for soldering electrical cables and why?
A resin type flux which is non-corrosive and will not attack the insulation on the cables.

77. Describe briefly how you would put a patch over a hole in a steel radiator-filler can.
(a) Cut a patch (of similar material to the can) a little larger than the hole. (b) Thoroughly clean the patch and an area around the hole about twice the area of the patch. (c) Apply flux to the cleaned sections. (d) Using a hot, cleaned and tinned iron, apply a thin coating of solder to the patch and to the part of the can to be covered by the patch (i.e. 'tin' the parts concerned). (e) Place the tinned patch in position over the hole and apply the hot iron until the solder on the two parts fuses together. (f) Do not disturb the patch until the solder sets. (g) Wash off any excess flux (if necessary).

SCREW THREADS, TAPS AND DIES

78. List the various principal types of screw thread in use on motor vehicles and give one typical example of where each may be found.
United States Standard (U.S.S.) or National Course (N.C.) is used on brass, bronze, aluminum and cast iron. Society of Automotive Engineers (S.A.E.) or National Fine (N.F.) threads are used in steel. Standard Pipe thread is used on brake lines, fuel lines and carburetor fittings.

79. For what are the following used? (a) Taps. (b) Stocks. (c) Dies.
(a) To cut internal screw threads. (b) To rotate the taps or dies. (c) To cut external screw threads.

80. Should taps and dies be used dry or lubricated?
Lubricated plentifully with light oil. Use soap and water when threading cast iron.

STEERING

81. What condition of steering geometry must the road wheels satisfy if they are to roll freely as the vehicle rounds a bend?
All the wheels must rotate about a common center.

82. How are the four wheels of a car made to 'rotate about a common center,' as mentioned in the previous question?
By means of the Ackerman steering layout.

83. Describe briefly the Ackerman steering layout.
With the front wheels pointing straight ahead, a line drawn through the center of one king-pin and track-rod-end ball joint, shall intersect a line drawn through the other king-pin and track-rod-end ball joint, at (or about) the center of the rear axle.

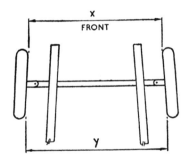

84. What is meant by the 'toe-in' of the front wheels?

This is where the road wheels are closer together at x than at y, as shown in the sketch above.

85. What would be the effect on the tires of excessive toe-in (or toe-out)?
Rapid tread wear. Increased fuel consumption.

BRAKES

86. Describe briefly the action of a simple hydraulic braking system when the pedal is depressed to apply the brakes.
When the pedal is depressed, fluid, being incompressible, must be displaced from the master-cylinder to some other part of the system. The only point at which the system can expand is in the wheel cylinders, where the pistons are forced outwards. Since the tips of the brake shoes bear on the wheel cylinder pistons, as these pistons move outwards, so the brake shoes are brought into contact with the drums.

87. **Virtually all vehicles produced today are equipped with hydraulically operated brakes. What are the advantages of such a system?**

(a) When the system becomes pressurized, i.e. when the brake pedal is depressed — an equal pressure is felt at all points in the system. Thus exactly equal braking effort can be applied to each wheel. The system is self-compensating. *(b)* Even if all the brake shoes are not adjusted equally near to the drum, braking effort will still be the same on all wheels. *(c)* Most parts of the system are self-lubricating, and hence wear rate is very low. *(d)* Hydraulic lines can easily be made to follow almost any desired path under the chassis. They do not have to go in straight lines as do most rod and cable brakes. *(e)* They are more weatherproof than mechanical systems and not prone to seize up. *(f)* If a differential braking action is required between front and rear brakes this can easily be achieved by using different sizes of wheel cylinders for front and rear. *(g)* Friction losses are low. *(h)* There are no rods to wear loose and rattle. *(i)* A high mechanical advantage can be obtained without the use of long levers. *(j)* No equalizer system is necessary. Pascal's law — A pressure on a liquid in a closed container is transmitted equally and undiminished in all directions.

88. **What are the disadvantages of hydraulic brakes?**

(a) The breakage of a brake line to one wheel, or any fault causing pressure loss, affects the complete hydraulic system (unless twin, or tandem, master cylinders are fitted). *(b)* If brake fluid leaks out on to the brake shoe lining, they will be ruined.

89. **What rule can be applied to determine which brake shoe is a primary shoe?**

A primary shoe is always the first shoe after the expander in the direction of drum rotation.

90. **Most modern cars with drum-type front brakes are designed so that both of the shoes on each front brake are primary shoes. How is this done?**

By providing an expander (wheel cylinder) for each brake shoe.

DRAWING

91. **List the minimum necessary drawing instruments required by a student of automobile engineering, assuming a drawing-board and "T" square are already available.**

45° set-square, 60°/30° set-square, 12-inch rule, compasses, rubber, 2H pencil, HB pencil, protractor.

92. What are the uses of the following types of lines in engineering drawings?

(A) —————————— Continuous (thick)

(B) —————————— Continuous (thin)

(C) -------------------------- Short dashes (thin)

(D) ₵ —–———–——– ₵ Long chain (thin)

(E) ～～～～～～ Continuous wavy (thick)

(F) —⌁——⌁——⌁— Ruled line and short zig-zgs.

(A) Visible outlines. (B) Dimension, projection, and section lines. (C) Hidden details. (D) Center lines. (E) Irregular boundary lines and short break lines. (F) Long break lines.

(Thick lines should be two to three times the thickness of thin lines.)

93. Show the following packing-piece in orthographic projection and name the views.

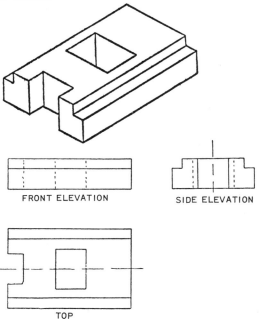

FRONT ELEVATION   SIDE ELEVATION

TOP

94. How would the flange shown below in pictorial view appear in section on A-A?

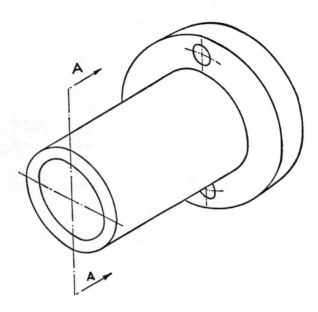

Flange shown in section on A-A.

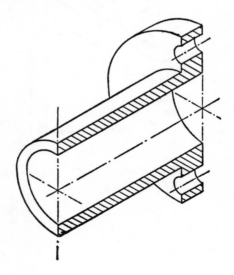

95. A blind "V" block is shown below in orthographic projection. How would it appear in isometric projection?

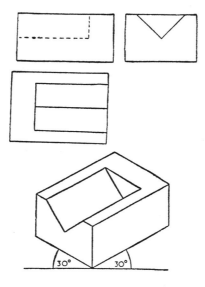

COOLING SYSTEM

96. With a conventional type of radiator, in which direction does the water flow?

The water enters at the top and leaves at the bottom.

97. What is the function of a thermostat?

It is a temperature sensitive valve which controls the rate of flow of water from the engine to the radiator and thus helps to maintain a constant engine operating temperature.

98. In a modern cooling system, besides its obvious function of closing the filler neck, the filler cap performs another important function. What is it?

The cap acts as a pressure valve to maintain the coolant under a slight pressure.

99. What is one very important reason for pressurizing the cooling system?

To increase the boiling point of the coolant.

100. What is the function of the water pump?
To give more positive and rapid circulation of the coolant.

CALCULATIONS, SCIENCE AND LABORATORY WORK
HEAT AND TEMPERATURE

101. Briefly explain the difference between temperature and heat.
Temperature is the degree of hotness or coldness of a body. It tells which way heat will flow (from that having higher to that having lower temperature).
Heat is a form of energy (and depends on weight as well as temperature).

102. Name the three ways in which heat may be transmitted.
Conduction, convection, and radiation.

103. Explain briefly the three ways of transmitting heat.
Conduction: heat travels through the material from the hotter to the colder part of the body.
Radiation: heat travels across an open space.
Convection: heat travels from one point to another by movement of gas or liquid.

104. *(a)* **How does a simple heated, bar-type electric windshield defroster cause air movement which helps to defog the windshield?** *(b)* **How does the heat escape from an engine cylinder (water-cooled)?** *(c)* **How is a motor-cycle engine cooled when the engine is running and the vehicle is stationary?**
(a) By convection currents set up in the air surrounding the hot defroster unit. *(b)* By conduction through the cylinder wall into the surrounding water-jacket. *(c)* By the heat being radiated from the fins into the surrounding air.

105. Place the following materials in order of thermal conductivity (heat transmission), the best first: wood, air, water, iron, copper, aluminum, and silver.
Silver, copper, aluminum, iron, wood, water, and air.

106. Give three cases in a motor vehicle where the expansion of metal when heated is used to advantage.

(a) Fitting starter ring gears. (b) Removing and fitting piston pins, in aluminum pistons. (c) Fitting bearing retaining rings.

107. Place the following metals in order of their expansion due to heat, the one which has the greatest expansion first: steel, aluminum, copper.

Aluminum, copper, steel.

108. Give an example of how the expansion and contraction of a liquid can be seen to be influenced by heat.

The water in an engine's cooling system (full when cold) expands when it is heated and small amounts of water may be seen coming out of the overflow. As the water cools (i.e. loses heat) it contracts; this can be seen by removing the filler cap and noting that the water level is low.

109. Give an example of where gas expands when heated and contracts when cooled.

If the tires of a car are at a certain pressure when cold and then the car is driven fast for a long distance, the tires heat up and the tire pressure rises. When the tires cool, however, the pressure returns to normal.

110. Two temperature scales are in common use. Name them and state the points on them corresponding to the freezing and boiling points of water.

Centigrade (Celsius): freezing-point 0°C and boiling-point 100°C, both at atmospheric pressure.

Fahrenheit: freezing-point 32°F and boiling-point 212°F, both at atmospheric pressure.

111. Convert a temperature reading of 77°F to °C.

$$°C = (°F - 32) \times \frac{5}{9}$$
$$= (77 - 32) \times \frac{5}{9}$$
$$= (45 \times \frac{5}{9})$$
$$= 25°C.$$

112. A water thermometer shows a temperature reading of 80°C. What would be the reading on a Fahrenheit thermometer?

$$°F = (°C \times \frac{9}{5}) + 32$$
$$= (80 \times \frac{9}{5}) + 32$$
$$= 144 + 32 \text{ or } 176°F.$$

FRACTIONS AND DECIMALS

113. Which is the numerator and which is the denominator of the following fraction? $\frac{7}{8}$.

7 is the numerator and 8 the denominator.

114. Give two examples of each of the following: *(a)* Proper fraction. *(b)* Improper fraction. *(c)* Mixed number.

 (a) $\frac{5}{8}$, $\frac{9}{16}$. *(b)* $\frac{9}{7}$, $\frac{17}{12}$. *(c)* $3\frac{1}{2}$, $15\frac{3}{16}$.

115. What is meant by the word 'of' in the following? $\frac{3}{4}$ of $\frac{1}{2}$.

'Of' means multiply. $\frac{3}{4} \times \frac{1}{2} = \frac{3}{8}$.

116. What is the rule to be followed when dividing by a fraction? Demonstrate its use to divide $\frac{3}{4}$ by $\frac{1}{2}$.

Invert (turn upside down) the divisor and multiply.

$$\frac{3}{4} \div \frac{1}{2} = \frac{3}{4} \times \frac{2}{1}$$
$$= \frac{6}{4}$$
$$= 1\frac{1}{2}$$

117. What is the overall length of this plate?

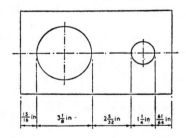

Overall length $= \frac{15}{16} + 3\frac{1}{8} + 2\frac{5}{32} + 1\frac{1}{4} + \frac{61}{64}$

$$= 6\ \frac{60 + 8 + 10 + 16 + 61}{64}$$
$$= 6\frac{155}{64}$$
$$= 8\frac{27}{64}\ \text{in.}$$

118. *(a)* How can a fraction be converted into a decimal? *(b)* Convert into decimals $\frac{3}{4}$ and $\frac{7}{8}$.

(a) Divide the numerator by the denominator.

(b) $\frac{3}{4}$ as a decimal = 3 ÷ 4 = 4)3.00

0.75

$\frac{3}{4}$ = 0.75

$\frac{7}{8}$ as a decimal = 7 ÷ 8 = 8)7.000

0.875

$\frac{7}{8}$ = 0.875

119. (a) How can a decimal be converted to a fraction? (b) Convert into fractions 0.25 and 0.625.

(a) Place the figure to be converted over a figure 1 and as many noughts as there are figures after the decimal point. Then reduce this fraction to its lowest terms by cancellation.

(b) 0.25 as a fraction = $\frac{25}{100}$ = $\frac{5}{20}$ = $\frac{1}{4}$

0.25 = $\frac{1}{4}$

0.625 as a fraction = $\frac{625}{1000}$ = $\frac{125}{200}$ = $\frac{25}{40}$ = $\frac{5}{8}$

0.625 = $\frac{5}{8}$

120. (a) When multiplying two decimal numbers together how is the position of the decimal point in the answer determined? (b) Evaluate 2.25 × 8.035.

(a) Count the number of figures behind the decimal points in the the numbers being multiplied, and in the answer place the decimal point that number of places from the right.

(b) 2.25 × 8.035

8.035) Number of figures after decimal points

2.25) = 5

16070
16070
41075

18.07875 point is placed after fifth figure from right.

Answer = 18.07875

121. Write down 60.0931 and 2.4835 correct to the third place of decimals.

60.093 ; 2.484.

122. What is the rule to be followed in similar questions to No. 121.

If the last figure is five or over, add one to the preceding figure. If the last figure is less than five ignore it.

PERCENTAGES AND APPROXIMATIONS

123. How is it possible to convert a fraction to a percentage?
Write down the fraction and multiply it by $\frac{100}{1}$.

124. During a road-worthiness test involving 200 vehicles, it was found that 86 had defective lights, 37 had defective steering, and 25 had defective brakes. What percentages do these represent?

Defective lights, percentage $= \frac{86}{200} \times \frac{100}{1} = 46\%$

Defective steering, percentage $= \frac{37}{200} \times \frac{100}{1} = 18.5\%$

Defective brakes, percentage $= \frac{25}{200} \times \frac{100}{1} = 12.5\%$

125. What is the approximate answer to the following sum?
$$\frac{21.735 \times 2.08 \times 1.401}{5.83}$$
Approximately this sum may be put down as:

$$\frac{21.735 \times 2.08 \times 1.401}{5.83} \simeq \frac{22 \times 2 \times 1.5}{6} = 11$$

Note $\simeq$ means 'approximately equal.'

WEIGHTS AND MEASURES

126. What are the commonly used U.S.A. units of lengths?
12 inches = 1 foot. 3 feet = 1 yard. 1760 yards = 1 mile.

127. What are the commonly used U.S.A. units of liquid measure?
2 pints = 1 quart. 4 quarts = 1 gallon.

128. List the commonly used U.S.A. units of weight.
16 ounces = 1 pound. 112 pounds = 1 hundredweight.
20 hundredweights = 1 ton; long ton no longer in use.

129. Answer the following: How many *(a)* **feet in 1 yard?** *(b)* **Yards in 1 mile?** *(c)* **Feet in 1 mile?** *(d)* **Pounds in 1 cwt?** *(e)* **Hundredweights in 1 ton?** *(f)* **Pounds in 1 ton?** *(g)* **Pints in 1 gallon?**
(a) 3. *(b)* 1760. *(c)* 5280. *(d)* 112. *(e)* 20. *(f)* 2000. *(g)* 8.

METRIC SYSTEM AND CONVERSIONS

130. **What are the units of length used in the metric system?**
10 millimetres = 1 centimetre. 10 centimetres = 1 decimetre.
10 decimetres = 1 metre. 10 metres = 1 decametre.
10 decametres = 1 hectometre. 10 hectometres = 1 kilometre.

131. **The most commonly used metric units of capacity (i.e. volume) are the cubic centimetre and the litre. What is their relationship to each other?**
1000 cubic centimetres = 1 litre.

132. **What are the two most widely used units of weight in the metric system and what is their relationship to each other?**
The gram and the kilogram.
1000 grams = 1 kilogram.

133. **How many centimetres (cm) are there in 1 inch, and how many millimetres (mm) are there in 1 inch?**
1 in. = 2.54 cm. 1 in. = 25.4 mm.

134. **How many millimetres equal 1 centimetre, and how many centimetres equal 1 metre (m)?**
10 mm. = 1 cm. 100 cm. = 1 m.

135. **A cylinder is 3.5 in. in diameter. Express this measurement in centimetres and millimetres.**
3.5 in. = 2.54 × 3.5 = 8.89 cm.
8.89 cm. = 8.89 × 10 = 88.9 mm.

136. **A valve is 15.875 cm. in length. Express this measurement in inches.**
15.875 cm. = 15.875 ÷ 2.54
= 6.25 in.

137. **An engine has a cubic capacity of 152 cubic inches. Given that 1 cubic inch = 16.5 cubic centimetres, what is the engine's capacity in cubic centimetres?**
Cubic centimetres = cubic inches × 16.5
= 152 × 16.5
= 2508 cm^3

THE AMERICAN GALLON AND SHORT TON

138. What is the relationship between the American (U.S.) gallon and the British or Imperial gallon?
1 U.S. gallon = 0.83 Imperial gallon.

139. The fuel tank of a car has a capacity of 12 Imperial gallons. How many U.S. gallons will it hold?

$$\text{U.S. gallons} = \frac{\text{Imperial gallons}}{0.83}$$

$$= \frac{12}{0.83} = 14.46 \text{ U.S. gallons}$$

140. What is the value of the 'short ton,' sometimes called the American ton?
1 short ton = 2000 pounds.

141. A vehicle weighs 4260 lb. What is its weight in 'short tons'?

$$\text{Short tons} = \frac{\text{weight in pounds}}{2000}$$

$$= \frac{4260}{2000}$$

$$= 2.13 \text{ short tons}$$

MENSURATION

142. Write down the formulae used to calculate the area of the following: *(a)* **Square or rectangle.** *(b)* **Triangle.**
(a) Area = length × breadth.
(b) Area = $\dfrac{\text{base} \times \text{perpendicular height}}{2}$

143. What are the formulae used to calculate: *(a)* **the circumference, and** *(b)* **the area of a circle?**
Let diameter = d and radius = r
(a) Circumference = πd or $2\pi r$

(b) Area = $\dfrac{\pi d^2}{4}$ or πr^2

144. Write down the value of π as a decimal and as a fraction.
$\pi = 3.142$; $\pi = 3\frac{1}{7}$ or $\frac{22}{7}$.

ANGLES AND TRIANGLES

145. How many degrees are subtended at the center of a circle?
360°.

146. Draw a right-angled triangle ABC with side AC and CB of equal length. Show which angle is the right angle and which side is the hypotenuse.

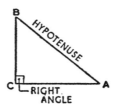

147. (a) How many degrees are there in a right angle? (b) What is the sum of the angle of a triangle?
(a) 90°. (b) 180°.

148. Complete the following table in respect of a right-angled triangle, lettered as shown in the previous question.
(a) Angle A = 60° angle B =
(b) Angle A =   angle B = 27°.
(c) Angle A = 12° angle B =
(a) A = 30°. (b) B = 63°. (c) B = 78°.

149. How many degrees are there in (a) 2 right angles, (b) $2\frac{1}{2}$ revolutions, (c) $\frac{1}{3}$ right angle, (d) 10 revolutions?
(a) 180°. (b) 900°. (c) 30°. (d) 3600°.

150. In any right-angled triangle what name is given to the longest side, and where will it always be found?
The longest side is the hypotenuse. It is the side opposite to the right-angle.

151. What is the theorem of Pythagoras, as concerning right-angled triangles?
The theorem of Pythagoras states: "The square of the hypotenuse of a right-angled triangle is equal to the sum of the squares of the other two sides."
$$C^2 = A^2 + B^2 \quad \text{thus} \quad C = \sqrt{A^2 + B^2}$$

FORCES

152. Define a 'force' and state in what units it is measured.

A force is that which changes or tends to change the state of motion or state of rest of a body. It is measured in any unit of weight, but generally in pounds or tons.

153. What are the three types of force? Give one example of each type when usefully applied to a piece of garage equipment.

(a) *Tensile:* a tow-rope is subject to tensile forces.

(b) *Compressive:* the pillars of a loaded vehicle hoist are subject to compressive forces.

(c) *Shear:* a guillotine shears the metal between its jaws.

WORK

154. Give a definition of work.

Work is said to be done when a force acting on a body causes it to move against a resistance in the direction of the force.

155. How can 'work done' be calculated?

Work done is the product of the applied force and the distance it moves in the direction of the force.

Work done = force applied × distance moved.

156. In what units is 'work done' measured?

The units used in its measurement are: foot-pound (ft/lb); foot-ton (ft/ton); inch-pound (in/lb); and inch-ton (in/ton).

The most widely used for automobile work being ft/lb.

POWER

157. What is power, and in what units is it measured?

Power is the rate of doing work. It is a measurement of the amount of work done in 1 minute, or 1 second.

Its unit of measurement is the horsepower (h.p.).

158. What does 1 horsepower represent in terms of (a) work done per minute; (b) work done per second?

(a) Work done at the rate of 33,000 ft/lb per min.

(b) Work done at the rate of 550 ft/lb per sec.

159. From the answers to the previous question, what two formulae can be made up to calculate horsepower?

$$\text{h.p.} = \frac{\text{work done per minute}}{33,000}$$

$$\text{h.p.} = \frac{\text{work done per second}}{550}$$

Work done to be in ft/lb.

160. A 12-V generator and alternator produces 30 amp. current. Find the wattage of the generator and alternator and the horsepower it absorbs from the engine (neglect the efficiency).

$$\text{Watts} = I \times E$$
$$= 30 \times 12$$
$$= 360 \quad (\text{Note: } 746 \text{ watts} = 1 \text{ horsepower.})$$

$$\text{Horsepower} = \frac{\text{watts}}{746}$$
$$= \frac{360}{746}$$
$$= 0.483.$$

GAS AND LIQUID FLOW

161. **Give one example of gas flow due to pressure difference.**
When the tire valve of an inflated tire is removed, air flows out of the tire (high pressure zone) into the surrounding atmosphere (low pressure zone).

162. **Give one example of liquid flow due to pressure difference.**
When a fuel pump diaphragm is operated so as to expand the internal volume of the pump (i.e. its 'suction' stroke), it creates a 'lower than atmospheric' pressure inside the pump. Fuel is forced from the tank, along the pipes, to fill up the pump chamber, because of the higher pressure (i.e. atmospheric pressure) now existing in the tank. The liquid flows from the high pressure region to the region of lower pressure.

CHANGE OF STATE AND MELTING POINTS OF METALS

163. **Give an example to show what is meant by the 'change of state' of a substance.**
When ice is heated, at 32°F it changes its state to become water; and when water is heater, at 212°F it changes its state and becomes steam.

164. Define briefly 'evaporation' and 'condensation.'
Evaporation: is when a liquid turns into a vapor.
Condensation: is when a vapor turns into a liquid.

165. What is the approximate melting-point of each of the following metals and alloys? *(a)* Solder. *(b)* White metal. *(c)* Aluminum. *(d)* Brass. *(e)* Cast Iron. *(f)* Mild steel.
(a) 428°F. *(b)* 680-1040°F. *(c)* 1220°F. *(d)* 1706°F. *(e)* 2192°F. *(f)* 2372°F.

FRICTION

166. Give four examples of places where friction is useful on a motor vehicle.
(a) Clutch. *(b)* Brakes. *(c)* Tires. *(d)* Fan belt.

167. Give four examples of where friction is undesirable on a motor vehicle.
(a) Engine bearings. *(b)* Between cams and their followers. *(c)* Between gear teeth. *(d)* Wheel bearings.

168. The packing-case shown weighs 100 lb, and in order to slide it across the floor a force of 60 lb is required. What is the coefficient of friction (μ) which exists between the case and the floor?

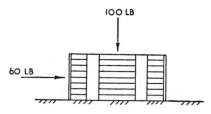

Let case weight = W and force required to overcome friction = F.

Then
$$\mu = \frac{F}{W} = \frac{60}{100}$$

Therefore
$$\mu = 0.6$$

169. If the case in Question 168 were now turned on end so that a much smaller area of it was in contact with the floor (μ remaining the same), would the force required to overcome friction be reduced? Give reasons for your answer.

No. The force required to overcome friction would remain the same, because friction is independent of area. $\mu = \dfrac{F}{W}$.

170. **What would be the desirability of, and the effect on, the frictional coefficients of introducing oil between** (a) **dry steel gear-teeth, and** (b) **brake linings and drum?**

(a) Frictional coefficient would be reduced to advantage.

(b) Frictional coefficient would be reduced to a dangerous level.

SIMPLE MACHINE

171. **The input movement in a simple machine (such as a lifting jack) bears a definite relationship to the output movement. What is this relationship called, and what formula may be used in its calculation?**

The relationship is known as the 'Movement Ratio' (or velocity ratio).

$$\text{Movement Ratio} = \frac{\text{movement at input}}{\text{movement at output}} .$$

172. **There is always an advantage in using a machine. With, e.g. a lifting jack, a small effort can be made to lift a large load. What is the name given to the ratio of the load divided by the effort?**

$$\text{Force ratio} = \frac{\text{load}}{\text{effort}}$$

Note: Force ratio is sometimes referred to as 'mechanical advantage.'

173. **By what two methods can the efficiency of a machine, expressed as a percentage, be worked out?**

$$\text{Efficiency of a machine} = \frac{\text{work output}}{\text{work input}} \times \frac{100}{1}$$

('Output' means work or power got out. 'Input' means work or power put in.)

$$\text{Efficiency of a machine} = \frac{\text{Force Ratio}}{\text{Movement Ratio}} \times \frac{100}{1}$$

174. **How is it possible to determine the speed ratio of a transmission (without dismantling)?**

(*a*) Select gear required.

(*b*) Mark input shaft and output shaft with chalk.

(*c*) Count number of revolutions of input shaft required to turn output shaft through one complete revolution; e.g. if input shaft must turn through 3 revolutions to rotate output shaft once, then movement ratio is 3 to 1 (usually written 3:1).

175. If a master gear and pinion were removed from a vehicle and found to have 35 teeth and 7 teeth respectively, how could their movement ratio be determined?

By using the following formula:

$$\text{Movement ratio} = \frac{\text{number of teeth on follower*}}{\text{number of teeth on driver†}}$$

$$= \frac{35}{7}$$

$$= 5:1$$

(* master gear; † pinion)

176. If a vehicle with a rear axle having a speed ratio of 5:1 was being driven in 2nd gear which had a ratio of 3:1, what would be the overall ratio?

Overall speed ratio = transmission ratio × rear axle ratio
$$= 3 \times 5$$
$$= 15:1$$

177. If the engine in the previous question was rotating at 3000 R.P.M., what would be the R.P.M. of the driving wheels?

$$\text{R.P.M. of driving wheels} = \frac{\text{engine R.P.M.}}{\text{overall speed ratio}}$$

$$= \frac{3000}{15}$$

$$= 200 \text{ R.P.M.}$$

178. The output shaft of a steering box cannot (usually) be rotated through a complete revolution. How then can its speed ratio be determined?

Note the number of turns of the steering wheel required to move the output shaft of the steering box through a measured number of degrees, e.g. if the steering wheel rotated four complete turns, whilst the output shaft rotated through 90° (one quarter of a revolution), then the ratio would be $4\frac{1}{4}$ or, more properly, 16:1.

LINEAR AND ROTATIONAL SPEEDS

179. Explain simply, what is meant by the linear and rotational speed of a driving wheel.

Linear speed — this is the speed at which a wheel travels along the ground. It may be measured in m.p.h. or ft per min., etc. Rotational speed — this is the number of revolutions the wheel makes in a certain time. It is usually measured in revolutions per minute (R.P.M.).

180. A wheel of diameter 21 in. rotates at 150 R.P.M. What will be its linear speed in feet per min.?

Linear speed = circumference in feet × R.P.M. (ft per min.)

$$= \frac{21}{12} \times \frac{22}{7}$$

$$= 825 \text{ ft per min.}$$

181. The linear speed of the rim of a pulley is 440 ft per min. If the pulley diameter is 4 in., what will be its speed in R.P.M.?

$$\text{R.P.M.} = \frac{\text{linear speed (in ft per min.)}}{\text{circumference (in ft)}}$$

$$= \frac{440}{(\pi D)/12}$$

$$= \frac{440 \times 7 \times 12}{4 \times 22}$$

$$\text{R.P.M.} = 420$$

182. An engine has a stroke of 4 in. and is rotating at 4500 R.P.M. What is the mean (i.e. average) linear speed at which the piston is travelling. Answer to be in feet per min.

Ft per min. Piston Speed = Stroke (in ft) × 2 × R.P.M.

$$= \frac{4}{12} \times 2 \times 4500$$

$$= 3000 \text{ ft per min.}$$

ELECTRICAL

FUNCTION OF MAIN COMPONENTS AND ELECTRICAL SYMBOLS

183. What are the functions of these main electrical parts of a

vehicle? (a) **Battery** (or accumulator). (b) **Generator** (or alternator). (c) **Ignition system.** (d) **Starter motor.**

(a) The battery stores (chemically) electrical energy, and supplies it to all other electrical units except the generator (or alternator).

(b) The generator (or alternator) generates electricity to recharge the battery.

(c) The ignition system provides the spark to fire the mixture in the cylinder.

(d) The starter is an electrical motor which rotates the engine and so obviates the need for hand-cranking.

184. **What do the following symbols represent?**

A: Lamp. B: Condenser. C: Ammeter. D: Fuse.

185. **Sketch the symbols used to represent the following:
A. 12-V battery showing positive and negative sides. B. Ground. C. Resistance. D. Wires crossing connected. E. Switch.**

COIL IGNITION SYSTEM

186. **What is the function of the coil ignition system?**

To provide, at the precise time it is required, the high voltage spark needed to 'jump' the plug gap inside the combustion chamber, in order to ignite the compressed mixture.

187. **In very simple terms how is the ignition spark produced?**

(a) The battery provides the initial source of low voltage electrical emergency.

(b) The ignition coil 'transforms' battery voltage current into the very high voltage current needed to jump the plug gap.

(c) The distributor acts as an automatic switch which times and distributes the spark to each cylinder in turn.

(d) The spark plug provides the gap inside the combustion chamber where the spark ignites the mixture.

SPARK PLUGS

188. How often should spark plugs be cleaned and their points re-gapped?

With normal-type plugs, about every 3000 to 5000 miles.

189. How should the points of a spark plug be re-gapped?

By bending the ground electrode only, either nearer to, or further away from, the center electrode, to obtain the recommended gap. The gap is best measured with a circular-section feeler gauge; alternatively, ordinary flat-bladed feelers may be used.

190. What should be the gap at the spark plug points?

This varies considerably according to the make and model of the engine, but is usually in the region of 0.020 inch to 0.040 inch.

191. Is it satisfactory to clean spark plugs with a wire brush?

No. They should be cleaned by sand blasting in order to remove carbon from the deep recess in the plug nose.

192. How should spark plugs be tested?

By means of a spark plug tester.

193. Spark plugs are sometimes tested by connecting up the plug lead, laying the plug on, for example, the cylinder head, and then cranking the engine with the ignition switched on, whereupon an apparently satisfactory spark occurs. Yet on being placed in the engine the plug sometimes still misfires. Why is this?

When the plug is being tested as described the insulating air gap between the plug points is only at atmospheric pressure. Under operating conditions the plug may have to operate at pressures well in excess of 100 p.s.i. This means that to jump across the gap the current must pass through a denser and hence better insulating layer of gas. Thus, if the voltage is not great enough, or the gap too wide, or if an easier path presents itself, the spark will not jump the gap.

194. Spark plugs should not be overtightened when fitted, but how can the correct amount of tightness be judged?

Insure the threads both on the spark plug and in the engine are clean, and use with a new plug washer. Screw in the plug by hand until it is finger tight on the washer. Tighten with torque wrench to manufacturers specifications.

ELECTRICAL UNITS, CONDUCTORS AND INSULATORS

195. State the units used for measuring the following electrical quantities: *(a)* **Pressure.** *(b)* **Current.** *(c)* **Resistance.**
(a) Volts. *(b)* Amperes. *(c)* Ohms.

196. *(a)* **What kinds of materials are good conductors?** *(b)* **What material is the best conductor?** *(c)* **What material is most commonly used as a conductor?**
(a) Metals and carbon. *(b)* Silver. *(c)* Copper.

197. **Make a list of five good insulators.**
(a) Air. *(b)* Glass. *(c)* Rubber. *(d)* Ebonite. *(e)* Oil.

ELECTRICAL CIRCUITS AND EFFECTS OF AN ELECTRIC CURRENT

198. **A 6-V lamp is connected to a 6-V battery. Draw two circuit diagrams to show the difference between two-wire (insulated-return) and common ground wiring.**

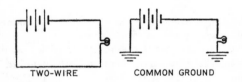

TWO-WIRE   COMMON GROUND

199. **Draw a circuit diagram showing two lamps connected in parallel across the terminals of a 6-V battery. Include a switch and an ammeter in the circuit (Common ground wiring).**

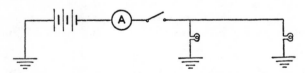

200. **Make the same circuit drawing as in the previous question, but this time with the lamps connected in series.**

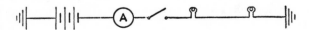

201. Are (almost all) lamps on a motor vehicle wired up in series or parallel?
In parallel.

202. Why is the common ground system almost universal on motor vehicles?
It is cheaper to install than insulated return and fault-finding is easier.

203. What are the three effects of an electric current? Give one example of each.
Chemical: battery. *Heating:* bulb filament. *Magnetic:* ignition coil.

204. What practical method can be used to measure the resistance of a conductor and in what units is electrical resistance measured?
By application of Ohm's law:

$$V = A \times R$$
$$A = V \div R$$
$$R = V \div A$$

SECOND YEAR

MOTOR VEHICLE TECHNOLOGY

CHASSIS LAYOUT

1. Commercial vehicle chassis side members are generally more straight and flat compared with those on a car (e.g. they may have no 'upsweep' over the rear axle). What are the advantages of this practice?

(a) The chassis becomes simpler and cheaper to make.

(b) It is easier to fit a specialist body to a simple shape of chassis.

2. A vehicle is said to have a conventional layout when fitted with a front-mounted engine driving the rear wheels. What other engine/drive arrangements are in common use?

(a) Front engine, front wheel drive. (b) Transverse front engine, front wheel drive. (c) Rear engine, rear wheel drive.

3. What are the advantages of rear-engined cars?

(a) Engine noise heard by the driver tends to be less and fumes are likely to be left behind. (b) Major mechanical units are compactly grouped and no long propeller shaft is required. (c) No propeller shaft tunnel intrudes into the passenger space. (d) Greater proportion of weight on rear wheels give a better grip on the road surface.

4. What are the disadvantages of rear-engined cars?

(a) Due to the concentration of weight at the rear, the back wheels can have a tendency to run wide on bends, i.e. oversteer. (b) Luggage space is usually smaller than in a conventional vehicle. (c) Engine, clutch, and transmission controls must be relayed through an extra distance. (d) Accessibility of major mechanical units is often poor.

5. What are the advantages of front-engined, front drive cars?

(a) Compactness of major mechanical units. (b) No propeller shaft tunnel means (usually) a low flat floor and low body line.

(c) Low body improves road holding. (d) Good traction round bends. (e) Extra weight on driving wheels improves their grip.

6. What are the disadvantages of front-engined, front drive cars?

(a) In most cases the drive to the steered wheels must be transmitted through complicated 'constant-velocity' universal joints. (b) A slight tendency to lose traction on very steep hills in slippery conditions. (c) Accessibility of transmission and final drive may be poor. (d) There may be a tendency towards heavy steering with perhaps the front end tending to run wide on bends, i.e. understeer.

LIMITS, FITS AND MEASURING

7. If a shaft is made to a size of 2.000 ± 0.001 in., what are the 'limits' of the shaft?

Top limit size is: Maximum possible shaft diameter = 2.001 in.
Bottom limit size is: Minimum possible shaft diameter = 1.999 in.

8. What is the 'tolerance' of the shaft mentioned in the previous question?

This is the margin of error between the maximum and minimum dimensions = $2.001 - 1.999 = 0.002$ in.

9. Give one example of an 'interference' fit, and one of a 'clearance' fit.

(a) Interference fit: dry cylinder in its cylinder block.
(b) Clearance fit: crankshaft in its bearings.

10. Mention five different tools used for measurement purposes when working on motor vehicles and state the approximate maximum degree of accuracy obtainable with each one.

(a) Feeler gauge, accuracy to 0.001 in.
(b) Vernier caliper, accuracy to 0.0001 in.
(c) Micrometer caliper, accuracy to 0.0001 in.
(d) Dial indicator micrometer, accuracy to 0.0001 in.
(e) Go no Go gauge, accuracy depending on skill of operator.

11. Give two examples of where an internal micrometer could be used.

(a) To measure the internal diameter of a cylinder bore.
(b) To measure the internal diameter of a main bearing.

12. A distance washer is 0.284 in. thick. Show a micrometer thimble and barrel set to the reading.

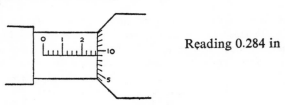

Reading 0.284 in

13. *(a)* What is the pitch of the spindle screw on a standard micrometer? *(b)* In what units is the barrel graduated? *(c)* How many divisions has the scale on the thimble and what fraction of an inch does each division represent?

(a) 0.025 in. *(b)* It is graduated in 1/10 in., and each 1/10 in. divided into four equal parts. Each division is thus 1/40 in. wide, i.e. 0.025 in. *(c)* 25 divisions, each representing 1/1000 in.

CYLINDER, CRANK AND VALVE ARRANGEMENTS

14. The cylinders of a four-cylinder engine are normally arranged in the in-line formation. Mention two other arrangements that are sometime employed.

(a) Horizontally opposed. *(b)* V-formation.

15. What cylinder arrangement is normally employed on an engine with three cylinders?

Three cylinders in-line.

16. Draw an end-on front view of a four-cylinder crankshaft to show the relative positions of the main and big-end journals. Indicate the interval in degrees between the crankpins.

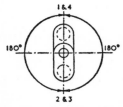

Four-cylinder Crankshaft

17. **Give two primary advantages of a four-cylinder V-engine over a conventional four-in-line engine.**

(*a*) Short power unit gives more passenger space.

(*b*) V-engine can be made lighter.

18. **Give two advantages of a flat-four engine over a four-cylinder in-line unit.**

(*a*) Very low overall height makes it particularly convenient for underfloor mounting. (*b*) Excellent engine balance (smoothness) is possible.

19. **Name, in order, from the camshaft to the valve, the various components of the valve operating gear of a push-rod operated overhead valve engine.**

Camshaft, cam-follower (or tappet), push-rod, rocker arm and valve.

20. **Name the main advantages of an overhead-valve engine, as opposed to a side-valve engine.**

(*a*) Greater accessibility. (*b*) Better filling of cylinders, as induction gas is helped down into the cylinders by the action of gravity, and ports can be made of better shape. (*c*) Cylinder block casting is less complicated. (*d*) Compression ratio can be made higher. (*e*) Design of combustion chamber more easily varied than with a side-valve engine.

21. **Name the main advantages of a side-valve engine as opposed to an overhead-valve engine.**

(*a*) Overall engine height can be low. (*b*) Less complicated head casting. (*c*) A side-valve engine generally retains its 'tune' longer than an overhead-valve unit, and shows greater tolerance of fuel. (*d*) No push-rods and rockers, etc., required to operate valves, therefore fewer moving parts. (*e*) Special valve-stem, oil-sealing arrangements not required.

22. **How would it be possible to measure accurately the 'lift' of a valve and compare this with crankshaft rotation?**

With the valve fully closed and its tappet clearance correct, fit a dial (probably with the aid of a magnetic base and stand), and zero the gauge with its measuring plunger resting on the valve (or something fixed to the valve, such as the spring plate). Fix a circular card, marked off in degrees, on to the flywheel face or crankshaft pulley. Rotate the engine slowly. Note the valve lift measured in thousandths of an inch and the corresponding movement of the flywheel measured in degrees. Plot the result on a graph.

CLUTCH AND TRANSMISSION

23. The illustration shows a Borg and Beck diaphragm spring clutch in the engaged position. What advantages has this type of clutch over the coil spring type clutch?

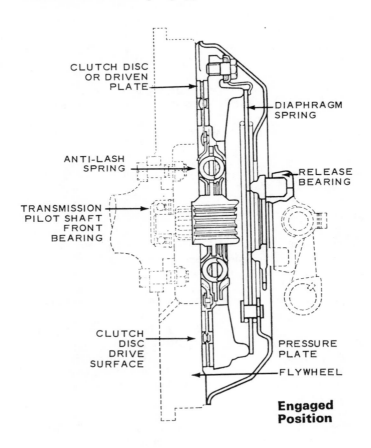

CLUTCH DISC
OR DRIVEN
PLATE

DIAPHRAGM
SPRING

ANTI-LASH
SPRING

RELEASE
BEARING

TRANSMISSION
PILOT SHAFT
FRONT
BEARING

CLUTCH
DISC
DRIVE
SURFACE

PRESSURE
PLATE

FLYWHEEL

**Engaged
Position**

(a) Lower operating effort. (b) Particularly suitable for high R.P.M. (c) This type of clutch is very compact, thus more torque and power can be transmitted within a given space. (d) More accurate balance is possible. (e) Much less prone to rattles and squeaks. (f) Virtually constant spring load throughout life of clutch.

24. The preceding question shows a clutch in the engaged (or driving) position. Explain what occurs on disengagement.

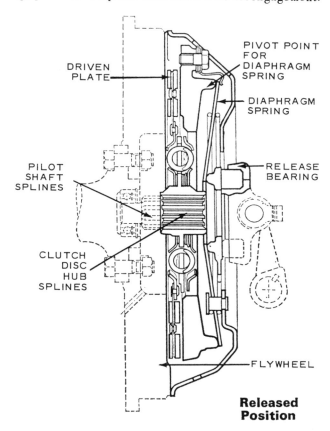

When the clutch pedal is depressed the release bearing moves inward towards the clutch, and the diaphragm spring assumes the shape shown below. This action withdraws pressure plate away from driven plate and drive is thus disengaged.

25. What is the general procedure for checking (on the bench) that a conventional coil-spring type clutch pressure plate assembly is correctly adjusted?

With the assembly secured to a clutch setting jig, determine that the inner tips of the release lever fingers are all at an equal height and are at the correct height for the clutch concerned.

26. **What is the essential difference between a sliding-pinion transmission and a constant mesh sliding-dog transmission?**

In the sliding pinion transmission, the actual gears themselves are caused to slide along the mainshaft to engage or disengage their respective mating gears on the cluster.

In the constant mesh type transmission, the cluster and mainshaft gears are in constant mesh. Since the mainshaft gears are designed to revolve freely on the main shaft, gear engagement is by sliding-dog-clutches splined to the mainshaft which lock the appropriate gear to the mainshaft in order that drive can take place.

27. **List in order, the various major components of a transmission, through which the power is transmitted when second gear is engaged.**

Clutch pilot shaft, clutch pilot shaft main drive pinion, cluster main drive pinion, cluster gear, second gear (cluster), second and high sliding gear, and mainshaft.

28. **If a conventional type transmission is in direct high drive state** (a) **which of the shafts are revolving and** (b) **the path by which the power is transmitted.**

(a) Clutch pilot shaft, cluster gear, mainshaft. (b) Clutch pilot shaft and mainshaft locked together by dog clutch.

29. **What is a common method of reversing the direction of rotation of the mainshaft of a transmission?** (i.e. obtaining reverse.)

By interposing a reverse idler gear between first and reverse sliding gear and cluster reverse drive gear.

PROPELLER SHAFT

30. **What is the purpose of the sliding joint on an open propeller shaft?**

When the rear axle rises and falls, because of spring deflection the distance between the axle and the transmission varies slightly. The sliding joint accommodates the necessary alterations in length of the propeller shaft.

31. **What is the function of propeller-shaft universal joints?**

When the car is moving on the road the rear axle, which is mounted on the springs, moves up and down relative to the transmission, which is secured to the chassis. Thus the angle of the propeller shaft is constantly altering. The universal joints allow the

drive to be transmitted through the varying (limited) angles assumed
by the shaft.

32. With some propeller shafts it is possible to separate them
into two parts at the sliding joint. When such a shaft is reassembled,
how is it possible to be sure that the universal joints are correctly
aligned?

(a) By means of two arrows, one on the outside of the internally
splined sleeve of the sliding joint and the other on the tube of the
propeller shaft itself at the end near to the external splines. These
arrows should be lined-up. (b) By fitting the sliding joint on the
splines so that the equivalent yokes at either end lie in the same
plane (i.e. are exactly in-line with one another).

33. How may an open-type propeller shaft be checked for
straightness?

Mount dial indicator on chassis or support close to propeller
shaft. Rotate shaft by hand and note run-out.

34. Name two makes of universal joint that may be used as a
propeller shaft.

'Hardy Spicer' universal coupling and the 'Layrub' flexible
coupling.

35. List the advantages the 'Layrub' type of flexible joint has
compared with the 'Hardy Spicer' type of joint.

(a) The rubber bushes allow the joint to act as a torsional vibration damper in the transmission system.

(b) The slight axial movement allowed by the rubber makes it
possible in some cases to dispense with the propeller shaft sliding
joint.

(c) The joint has no moving parts and therefore requires no
lubrication.

(d) Transmission noise is not as easily transmitted along the
shaft.

36. List the advantages of an all-metal joint, such as the 'Hardy-
Spicer,' compared with a flexible joint of the 'Layrub' type.

(a) The all-metal joint can be used for greater angular deflections.

(b) The overall dimensions of the joint are less.

(c) Satisfactory balance is more likely to be obtained, particularly
at high R.P.M.

37. What type of bearing is used in the 'Hardy Spicer' joint?

Because of the limited angular movement and to prevent "grooving" of the race, needle roller bearings are used. They keep down the weight and the size of the joint and can also function for long periods with the minimum of lubrication.

REAR AXLE AND FINAL DRIVE

38. Name three types of rear-axle reduction gears.

(a) Spiral-toothed bevel. (b) Hypoid. (c) Worm.

39. Give one typical example of where each of the gears mentioned in the answer to the previous question might be found. State also the approximate gear ratio that would be used.

(a) *Spital-toothed bevel gear:* Light or medium-sized older car. Gear ratio 5:1.

(b) *Hypoid gear:* Medium commercial vehicle. Gear ratio 7:1. Also medium-sized modern car. Gear ratio 4:1.

(c) *Worm gear:* Heavy commercial vehicle. Gear ratio 12:1.

40. What are the advantages and disadvantages of spiral-toothed bevel rear-axle gears?

Advantages: (a) Cheapness. (b) Quietness of running. (c) Fairly easy to set up. (d) Do not require special lubricant.

Disadvantages: (a) Not suitable for gear ratios below about 5:1. (b) The pinion can only enter along the center line of the master gear. Thus a low propeller shaft line is not possible.

41. What are the advantages of hypoid rear-axle gears?

(a) Very quiet running. (b) Pinion is offset below the center of the master gear. This gives lower propeller shaft, thus allowing a flatter car floor or lower body. (Pinion can be offset above the center of the master gear.) (c) Pinion is larger and teeth are stronger, resistance to fatigue is high, more teeth in constant mesh. (d) Ratios as low as approximately 7.25:1 can be obtained, gives a lower center of gravity. (e) Larger pinion allows the use of larger pinion bearings. (f) Long life.

42. What are the disadvantages of hypoid gears?

(a) They are expensive to produce. (b) Special lubricant is required. (c) Setting-up is often difficult and requires the use of special tools.

43. Why is it that special lubricant is required for hypoid gears?
Because of the shape of the gear teeth, the action as they mesh is partly rolling and partly sliding. The sliding produces extremely high local pressures between the teeth, which means that special 'extreme pressure' lubricant must be employed.

44. Whereabouts in a rear axle are oil seals normally located?
(a) One in the nose of the pinion housing. (b) One at each end of the axle shaft housing to prevent lubricant reaching the brakes.

45. Rear axles are normally classified in accordance with the method of supporting the axle shaft in the casing. What are the names of the three types?
(a) Semi-floating axle. (b) Three-quarter-floating axle. (c) Fully-floating axle.

46. How can the individual types of rear axle mentioned in the previous question be most easily defined and recognized?
(a) *Semi-floating:* one bearing fitted inside the axle case.
(b) *Three-quarter-floating:* one bearing fitted on outside of axle case.
(c) *Fully-floating:* two bearings fitted a little distance apart on the outside of the axle base. Axle shaft may be removed without removing wheel. Axle shaft has no function but' to supply power to drive wheels.

47. Which two types of axle mentioned above are normally used on private cars?
Semi-floating and full-floating (jeeps, four-wheel drive vehicles and front drive vehicles).

48. What is the purpose of the differential?
To allow the driven road wheels to rotate at different speeds as required, but at all times with equal torque.

STEERING

49. Name four types of steering gear in general use.
(a) Recirculating ball. (b) Worm and sector. (c) Rack-and-pinion. (d) Cam-and-peg.

50. What would be a typical sequence of operations needed to dismantle a simple steering box? (Assuming the assembly has already been removed from the vehicle and has had the steering wheel removed.)

(a) Drain off the oil. (b) Remove the Pitman arm. (c) Take off the top cover and withdraw the cross-shaft. (d) Remove the bottom plate and withdraw the steering shaft.

51. Mention three places on a steering shaft at which adjustment might be found and state the type of adjustment.

(a) Bolt and lock-nut on top cover plate. (b) Shims under top cover plate. (c) Shims under end plate.

BRAKES

52. Name two types of braking system in common use.

(a) Hydraulic. (b) Mechanical.

53. Briefly describe the principle of (a) drum brakes and (b) disc brakes.

(a) When the brake pedal is depressed, friction-material-faced brake shoes move outwards into contact with the drum to provide the braking effort. (b) When the brake pedal is depressed, pads of friction material are forced towards one another and in so doing come into contact with the disc which normally rotates between them.

54. What is the usual method of gaining access to drum-type brakes?

With the car safely jacked-up, remove the wheel, release the handbrake, undo the drum securing screws, and slide the drum outwards off the wheel studs.

55. What would be the effects of a dragging brake?

(a) Rapid lining (or pad) wear. (b) Overheating of braking surfaces and possibly hub. (c) Engine will appear to pull badly and fuel consumption will increase.

56. What would be the effect of excessive clearance between the lining and the drum (or pad and disc)?

Brake pedal travel would be increased and effective pedal leverage reduced.

CALCULATIONS, SCIENCE AND LABORATORY WORK

GRAPHS

57. What sensible rules should be observed when making up a graph?

(a) Choose a sensible scale that will be easy to read and as large as convenient on the paper available. (b) The names of the two scales (e.g. horsepower, time, weight, etc.) must be shown. (c) The graph should have a title. (d) Plot the points in pencil and lightly draw in the curve to see that it conforms with the expected shape, preparatory to finalizing the graph. Any points well out of the general run of the curve should be double checked for accuracy. (e) If more than one curve appears on a graph label each one.

58. **If, when plotting a graph of say an engine test, many of the points lie a little above or below the path which would produce a smooth curve, what is the procedure to follow?**

Draw a smooth curve through the mean (or average) position of the various points.

59. **Is it necessary to show on the graph the table of results or information from which a graph was plotted?**

No, not unless specifically requested to do so.

DENSITY

60. **What simple formula is used to determine the density of a substance?**

$$\text{Density} = \frac{\text{Weight}}{\text{Volume}}$$

61. **A rectangular block of brass measures 4 in. × 3 in. × 2 in. and weighs 7.2 lb. What is its density in pounds per cubic inch?**

$$\text{Density} = \frac{\text{weight}}{\text{volume}}$$

$$= \frac{7.2}{4 \times 3 \times 2}$$

$$= \frac{7.2}{24}$$

$$= 0.3 \text{ lb per in}^3$$

62. **How can the relative densities of different liquids be determined?**

Weigh *equal volumes* of each liquid in turn. The greater the weight (of a given volume) then the greater is its density.

63. **What is meant by the 'specific gravity' of a substance?**

This is the ratio of the weight of any volume of the substance compared to the weight of an equal volume (in the case of solids and liquids) of water.

64. **What formula can be used to determine the specific gravity of a substance?**

$$\text{Specific gravity} = \frac{\text{weight of substance}}{\text{weight of equal volume of water}}$$

65. **Give two practical applications of where it may be necessary to determine the specific gravity of a substance when working in a garage.**

(a) To determine the state of charge of a battery.

(b) Testing the strength of antifreeze solution.

EFFECT OF TEMPERATURE, VOLUME, AND PRESSURE CHANGES ON GASES

66. **When a gas, air for example, is compressed, it heats up. Explain very briefly how one type of automotive engine makes use of this phenomenon.**

The compression ignition (diesel) engine, uses the heat generated during the compression stroke, to ignite the fuel injected into the cylinder.

67. **Mention one obvious and practical way in which the pressure of a gas can be shown to have increased due to temperature rise.**

The tire pressures of a car increase noticeably when the tire heats up, as say after a period of high speed running.

68. **How can it be demonstrated that when the volume of a gas is reduced, that its pressure rises?**

By inserting a pressure gauge into the spark plug hole of an engine and bring the piston from b.d.c. to t.d.c. on the compression stroke. The rising piston effectively reduces the volume of gas present and the pressure gauge will indicate a rise in pressure.

STRESS AND STRAIN

69. **List three motor vehicle components that are subjected to tensile stress.**

(a) Cylinder head studs. (b) Handbrake cables. (c) Fan belt.

70. List three motor vehicle components that are subjected to compressive stress.

(a) Plain washers under say cylinder head nuts. (b) Cylinder head gasket. (c) Pedal rubbers as driver puts his feet on them.

71. What formula is used to calculate: (a) tensile stress; (b) shear stress; (c) compressive stress?

The same formula is used for all these:

$$\text{Stress} = \frac{\text{load}}{\text{area resisting load}}$$

where load is measured in pounds or tons, and area in square inches.

72. A garage crane is lifting a load of 2000 lb. The hook is made of circular section steel bar with a cross sectional area of 0.5 in², whilst the steel chain above the hook has an effective cross sectional area of 0.25 in². Which component (the hook of the chain — which are both supporting the same load) is subject to the greater stress, or are both subject to an equal stress?

The chain is subjected to the greater stress.

73. Using the information given in the previous question, prove that the answer given is correct.

$$\text{Stress} = \frac{\text{load}}{\text{area resisting load}}$$

Hook:
$$\text{Stress} = \frac{\text{load}}{\text{area}}$$

$$= \frac{2000}{0.5}$$

$$= 4000 \text{ lb per in}^2$$

Chain:
$$\text{Stress} = \frac{\text{load}}{\text{area}}$$

$$= \frac{2000}{0.25}$$

$$= 8000 \text{ lb per in}^2$$

74. A bearing cap is secured by two 3/8-in. diameter B.S.F. bolts with a core diameter of 0.311 in. Find the stress in the bolts when the cap is subjected to a load of 2000 lb.

$$\text{Stress} = \frac{\text{load}}{\text{area resisting load}}$$

$$= \frac{2000}{\text{combined cross-sectional area of bolts}}$$

$$= \frac{2000}{2\left\{\dfrac{\pi \times 0.311 \times 0.311}{4}\right\}}$$

$$= \frac{2000 \times 7 \times 4}{2 \times 22 \times 0.311 \times 0.311}$$

$$= 13,160 \text{ lbs p.s.i.}$$

Note: Bolt cross-sectional area is calculated on the core diameter.

75. A force of 10 ton is needed to punch a 2-in. diameter hole out of a plate 1/8 in. thick. Calculate the shear strength of the material to the nearest 100 lbs p.s.i.

$$\text{Strength} = \text{resistance to stress}$$

$$\text{Stress} = \frac{\text{load}}{\text{area resisting load}}$$

$$= \frac{10 \times 2240}{\text{circumference of hole} \times \text{metal thickness}}$$

$$= \frac{10 \times 2240}{\pi \times 2 \times \frac{1}{8}}$$

$$= \frac{7 \times 10 \times 2240 \times 8}{22 \times 2 \times 1}$$

$$= 28,500 \text{ lbs p.s.i.}$$

76. A $3\frac{1}{2}$-in. diameter bore oil engine has a maximum cylinder pressure of 600 lbs p.s.i. If the cross-sectional area of the connecting rod is $\frac{3}{4}$ in^2 what will be the maximum compressive stress in the rod?

$$\text{Stress} = \frac{\text{load}}{\text{area resisting load}}$$

$$= \frac{\text{piston area} \times \text{pressure per in}^2}{\frac{3}{4}}$$

$$= \frac{\pi \times 3\frac{1}{2} \times 3\frac{1}{2}}{4} \times 600 \div \frac{3}{4}$$

$$= \frac{22 \times 7 \times 7 \times 600 \times 4}{7 \times 2 \times 2 \times 4 \times 3}$$

$$= 7700 \text{ lbs p.s.i.}$$

77. What is strain?

This is the change in shape (which may be extremely slight) of a component, due to stress.

Note: *All* vehicle components are stressed to a greater or lesser degree, but in the majority of cases the strain is not obvious.

78. Give two examples, one compressive and one tensile, of how stress in a component produces strain.

(a) The firing thrust on top of the piston imparts a compressive stress to the connecting rod, which then (momentarily) shortens in length. (b) As the handbrake is applied the tensile stress in the cable causes it to expand slightly (and temporarily) in length.

79. What formula is used to calculate strain?

$$\text{Strain} = \frac{\text{Change in length}}{\text{Original length}}$$

Note: Both lengths must be in the same units, usually inches.

80. In an experiment, a 5-ft length of steel cable is subject to a tensile load which stretches by 0.012 in. Calculate the strain.

$$\text{Strain} = \frac{\text{increase in length}}{\text{original length}}$$
$$= \frac{0.012}{5 \times 12}$$
$$= 0.0002$$

81. If in the previous experiment the length of the cable had been doubled whilst the load remained the same, what would have been the effect on stress in the cable.

It would not alter.

VOLUMES AND WEIGHTS OF RECTANGULAR SOLIDS AND CYLINDERS

82. A rectangular packing-case measures 12 ft × 4 ft × 3 ft. What is its volume?

$$\text{Volume} = \text{length} \times \text{width} \times \text{height}$$
$$= 12 \times 4 \times 3$$
$$= 144 \text{ ft}^2$$

83. The bore and stroke of an oil engine are 3.5 in. and 4 in. respectively. Find the cylinder volume in cubic inches.

Volume of cylinder = area of the end × length

$$= \frac{\pi d^2}{4} \times 4$$

$$= \frac{22}{7} \times \frac{3.5 \times 3.5}{4} \times 4$$

$$= 38.5 \text{ in}^3$$

84. A rectangular section mild steel packing piece measures 3 in. × 2 in. × 1½ in. If the steel has a density of 0.28 lb per in³, what will be the weight of the piece?

Weight = volume × density

$$= 3 \times 2 \times 1\frac{1}{2} \times 0.28$$

$$= 2.52 \text{ lb}$$

85. A circular-section fuel tank is 2 ft 6 in. long and the area of its end is 2 ft². Find the weight of fuel it can contain if 1 gallon of the fuel weighs 8 lb. (1 ft³ = 6.25 gal.)

Volume of tank = length × area of end

$$= 2.5 \times 2$$

$$= 5 \text{ ft}^3$$

Number of gal. = Number of cubic feet × gallons per cubic foot

$$= 5 \text{ ft}^3 \times \text{gal}/\text{ft}^3$$

$$= 31.25$$

Weight = Number of gallons × weight of 1 gallon

$$= 31.25 \text{ gal.} \times 8 \text{ lb}$$

$$= 250 \text{ lb}$$

TORQUE

86. Define 'torque.' In what units is it normally measured?

Torque is a turning or a twisting moment. It is measured in foot lbs, or, for small amounts, in inch lbs.

87. How can the value of a torque or turning moment be calculated?

It is the product of the applied force and the perpendicular radius at which it is acting.

Torque = force × radius.

88. What is the formula used to calculate the work done by a torque?

Work done by a torque = force applied × distance force moves

or

Work done by a torque = $2\pi NT$

where N = number of revolutions

T = torque

89. List five types of important nuts (or bolts), that should be tightened using a torque wrench.

Those which secure: *(a)* cylinder heads, *(b)* connecting rod bearing nuts, *(c)* spring 'U' bolts, *(d)* main bearings, *(e)* wheels, spark plugs, manifolds, clutch housing and all parts specified by the manufacturer.

FREEZING AND BOILING POINTS

90. What are the freezing and boiling points of water in *(a)* degrees Centigrade and *(b)* degrees Fahrenheit?

(a) 0°C and 100°C. *(b)* 32°F and 212°F.

91. What principle factor determines the freezing point of an ordinary (ethylene glycol) type antifreeze?

The antifreeze/water proportion.

92. The usually recommended antifreeze/water solution is 25 per cent by volume. What frost protection will this solution afford?

The mixture will remain free-flowing down to 9°F and will not freeze solid until −15°F.

93. At what temperature would the antifreeze/water solution mentioned in the previous question, start to boil?

219°F.

94. At what temperature will the electrolyte in a battery freeze?

This depends upon the state of charge of the battery. For example, a fully charged battery with a specific gravity reading of 1.300 would not freeze until the temperature fell to −76°F, whilst a discharged battery with a specific gravity of 1.100 would freeze at 9°F.

95. Unlike water which has a precise boiling temperature, gasoline boils between about 86°F and 356°F. What is the reason for this wide boiling range?

Gasoline is a mixture of many compounds, and various 'fractions' of the gasoline have various boiling points.

MOVEMENT AND TORQUE RATIOS

96. How would it be possible to determine the overall movement ratio (gear ratio) between an engine and the driving wheels?

(a) Jack up the driving wheels, (b) engage the selected gear, (c) rotate the engine until *both* rear wheels had revolved only once and note the number of turns of the starting handle.

97. If in the previous question, the overall gear ratio (in direct drive 'high' gear) was found to be 4.5:1, what would be the torque at the driving wheels if the engine was delivering 50 ft. lbs. torque? (Neglect friction)

Torque at driving wheels = engine torque × overall gear ratio
$$= 50 \times 4.5$$
$$= 225 \text{ ft. lbs.}$$

98. If a clutch pedal was depressed 6 in., while the end of the clutch arm acting on the release lever moved ½ in., what would be the movement ratio?

$$\text{Movement ratio} = \frac{\text{movement at input}}{\text{movement at output}}$$
$$= \frac{6}{\frac{1}{2}}$$
$$= 12:1$$

99. If with the clutch mentioned in the previous question, the driver applied a force of 30 lbs to the clutch pedal, what would be the resulting force on the release bearing?

Load on release bearing = pedal load × movement ratio
$$= 30 \times 12$$
$$= 360 \text{ lbs.}$$

LINEAR AND ANGULAR SPEEDS, AND ACCELERATION

100. If an engine with a 3-in. stroke was rotating at 2500 R.P.M., what would be the linear speed in feet per minute of the pistons?

Piston speed = R.P.M. × distance travelled by piston during 1 revolution of crank.

(Note: In one revolution of crank, piston travels both down and up
the stroke.)

$$\text{Piston speed} = 2500 \times \frac{3 \times 2}{12} = 1250 \text{ ft per min.}$$

**101. By reference to the piston mentioned in previous question,
explain the difference between acceleration and speed.**

The piston is at a (momentary) standstill at t.d.c. and b.d.c. and
then accelerates rapidly to achieve its maximum speed about half
way along its stroke.

See also 'First Year' Questions 179 to 182.

METALS UNDER LOAD

**102. Place the following metals in their order of strength as
when subjected to tensile loading; cast iron, steel, and aluminum
(strongest first).**

Steel, aluminum, cast iron.

**103. Which one of the metals in the previous question has (within
its elastic limits) the greatest resistance to constant reversals
of load?**

Cast iron.

**104. Which of the three metals just mentioned has the greatest
strength when subjected to compressive forces?**

Steel.

ELECTRICAL

OHM'S LAW AND VOLTAGE DROP

**105. The relationship between the three fundamental electrical
units is known as Ohm's law. State this law.**

Ohm's law says: In an electrical circuit the current flowing in
amperes is proportional to the potential difference in volts divided
by the resistance in ohms.

**106. To assist in remembering the formula associated with
Ohm's law the diagram shown is sometimes used. What do the
letters stand for and how can this diagram be used?**

E = Voltage (volts)
I = Current (amperes)
R = Resistance (ohms)

To use the diagram, cover up whichever letter is required to be the subject of the formula. The remaining two letters will be in their correct relative positions. Thus:

$$E = I \times R, \quad I = \frac{E}{R}, \quad R = \frac{E}{I}.$$

107. What is meant by 'voltage drop' or 'fall of potential' in respect of current flowing in electrical cables? Give one example of where this obviously occurs.

The current leaving the battery may be 12V, yet the current at the starter motor may well only be of the order of 10V. The 2V loss of voltage occurs due to the resistance to current flow offered by the starter cable.

108. Using Ohm's law, calculate the resistance of the cable mentioned in answer to the previous question if the current flowing to the starter motor was 100 amps.

$$R = \frac{E}{I}$$
$$= \frac{2}{100}$$
$$= 0.02 \text{ ohms}$$

Note: Value of E in this case is value of volt drop.

BULBS, LAMPS AND WIRING

109. State the likely wattage ratings for the bulbs in the following list of lamps, if they were intended for use on a private car with a 12V electrical system. Side, head, stop, fog and panel lights.

Side 6W. Head 60W. Stop 21W. Fog 48W. Panel 3W.

110. What would be the value (measured in amperes) of the current required by each of the bulbs in the previous question?

$$\text{Amperes} = \frac{\text{Watts}}{\text{Volts}}$$

Therefore current flowing in each bulb is found as follows:

6W Side lamp, $\dfrac{6}{12} = 0.5$ amps.

60W Head lamp, $\dfrac{60}{12} = 5$ amps.

21W Stop lamp, $\dfrac{21}{12}$ = 1.75 amps.

48W Fog lamp, $\dfrac{48}{12}$ = 4 amps.

3W Panel lamp, $\dfrac{3}{12}$ = 0.25 amps.

111. How can headlamp alignment be checked?

(a) By means of beamsetting equipment, or (b) as shown in diagram.

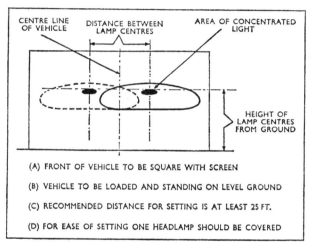

CENTRE LINE OF VEHICLE   DISTANCE BETWEEN LAMP CENTRES   AREA OF CONCENTRATED LIGHT

HEIGHT OF LAMP CENTRES FROM GROUND

(A) FRONT OF VEHICLE TO BE SQUARE WITH SCREEN

(B) VEHICLE TO BE LOADED AND STANDING ON LEVEL GROUND

(C) RECOMMENDED DISTANCE FOR SETTING IS AT LEAST 25 FT.

(D) FOR EASE OF SETTING ONE HEADLAMP SHOULD BE COVERED

112. What is the most commonly used headlamp anti-dazzle device?

Double-filament bulbs. The main-beam filament is positioned at the focal point of the reflector, whilst the dipped-beam filament (usually of lower wattage) is offset from the focal point. This offset results in the light from the dipped-beam filament being distributed more sharply downwards and displaced towards the nearside.

113. What would be a suitable wiring arrangement for a fog-lamp?

With the wiring arrangement shown on the next page the lamp cannot be inadvertently left on after the side lamps have been extinguished.

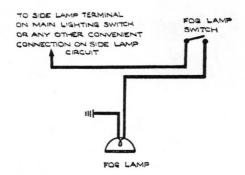

TO SIDE LAMP TERMINAL
ON MAIN LIGHTING SWITCH
OR ANY OTHER CONVENIENT
CONNECTION ON SIDE LAMP
CIRCUIT

FOG LAMP
SWITCH

FOG LAMP

114. What would be a suitable wiring arrangement for a reversing light?

See diagram below:

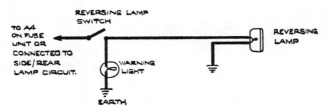

REVERSING LAMP
SWITCH

TO A4
ON FUSE
UNIT OR
CONNECTED TO
SIDE/REAR
LAMP CIRCUIT.

WARNING
LIGHT

REVERSING
LAMP

EARTH

115. How is it possible to tell quickly and easily (without dis-
connecting any terminals) how much current there is flowing in any
particular cable?

By means of an 'induction type' ammeter which clips loosely on
to the outside of the cable (at any convenient point along its length).
The magnetic field set up by the current passing through the cable
is sufficient to operate this type of meter.

116. What are the names and typical uses of the terminals
shown below?

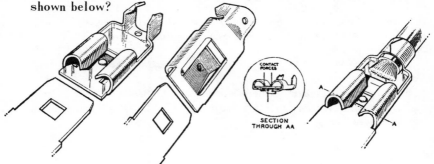

CONTACT
FORCES

SECTION
THROUGH AA

117. What is the name of the type of terminal shown below and how is the bared copper wire secured to it?

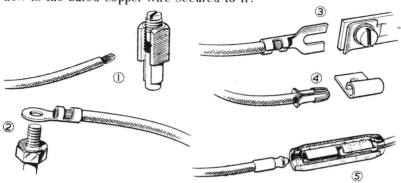

118. The electric cables of a car are usually differently colored. Why is this?

In order to make it easier to trace circuits — e.g. when the vehicle is undergoing repair.

119. Tracer colors are sometimes added to cables. What are these? Give an example of their use.

When a cable with a certain basic color has one or more different colors added, these are called tracer colors. For example, the lead to a headlamp main-beam filament may be blue only, while the lead to the dipped filament may have a basic color of blue with a tracer color of red.

All the various wires making up a wiring harness have different color combinations.

120. How are automobile cable sizes designated?

Wire and cable sizes are expressed by a gauge number which indicates the cross-sectional area (not diameter) of the conductor. The cross-sectional area of wires is given in circular mils. (A circular mil is a unit of area equal to the area of a circle one mil in diameter. A mil is a unit of length equal to 0.001 inch. Thus a wire 10 mils in diameter has a cross-sectional area of 100 circular mils or 78.54 sq. mils).

In the case of cables, which are made up of a number of strands of wire, the cross-sectional area of the cable is equal to the circular mil area of a single wire multiplied by the number of strands in the cable.

121. What are typical cable-wire sizes of various applications?

Lighting — In order to conserve current, lighting wire must be of adequate size. The voltage loss in a length of wire is equal to the product of the current flowing and the resistance of the wire. Keeping the resistance of the wire to a minimum will keep the voltage drop (*IR* drop) to a minimum. Since the resistance of a length of wire decreases as its diameter increases, it is advisable to use wire of relatively large cross section. In general no wire smaller than 16 gauge should be used for small candle power lights while headlights and accessories will require a larger gauge wire.
Note: the larger the gauge number the smaller the wire diameter.

Cables — Since the cranking motor will draw approximately 250 amps it is necessary that the cable between the battery and cranking motor be of sufficient gauge to carry this heavy current. For this reason #1 or #2 gauge cable must be used.

COIL IGNITION SYSTEM

122. Show, by means of a line diagram, a coil ignition system layout for a 6-cylinder engine.

See diagram on next page.

123. The ignition system is made up of two separate circuits. What are their names and how are they distinguished?

Primary circuit and secondary circuit, sometimes known as 'low tension' and 'high tension' circuits respectively. Primary circuit, composed of battery, ignition switch, contact points, condenser (capacitor), ignition coil and primary wiring. Secondary circuit, composed of distributor cap, rotor, ignition coil, high tension wiring and spark plugs.

124. Briefly and simply, how does the coil ignition system work?

With the contact-breaker points closed, current flows through the primary circuit. When the points are opened (by the cam) current can no longer flow in the primary circuit and at this moment the ignition coil produces a high voltage current. This high voltage current flows from the center terminal of the coil, via the heavily insulated leads, to the rotor arm. From there it jumps on to whichever cap segment the rotor arm is opposite, and then travels along the connecting lead to the spark plug, where it jumps to ground across the points and there provides the spark.

125. What is the voltage of the primary-circuit current?

Battery voltage.

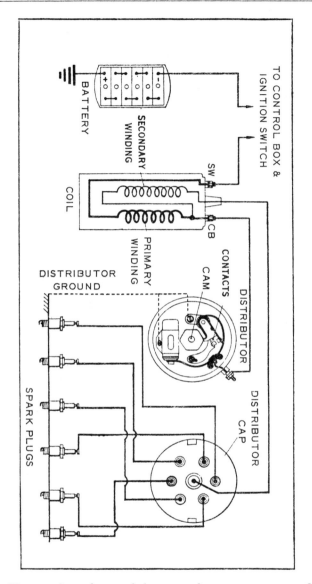

126. What is the voltage of the secondary-circuit current?

It can vary widely, but it is approximately between 8000 volts and 20,000 volts.

127. What is the function of the condenser?

To minimize arcing at the contact-breaker points and to improve the quality of the high-tension spark; to cause a quick collapse of the magnetic field of the coil core.

128. What is the purpose of the contact-breaker points?

These, together with their operating cam, form an automatic switch, timed to the engine, which controls the flow of current through the primary circuit and the timing of the high-tension spark.

129. What is the purpose of the carbon brush in the distributor cap, and why is this brush always made of carbon?

It conveys the high-tension current from the stationary cap to the moving rotor arm. It must under these circumstances be both a suitable conductor for the current and a dry lubricant in itself.

130. At what speed is the distributor driven on a four-stroke engine? Why is it driven at that speed?

(a) The distributor is driven at half engine speed (i.e. camshaft speed). (b) It is usual to have one cam lobe for each cylinder. As each cylinder fires only once in every two revolutions, a particular cam lobe for a particular cylinder need only open the contact-breaker points once in two revolutions of the engine. Thus the distributor need be driven at only half the speed of the crankshaft.

BATTERIES

131. What is the function of a battery (or accumulator) of the type used on a motor vehicle?

The battery stores (chemically) electrical energy and supplies it to all other electrical units except the generator-alternator.

132. Explain simply the difference between primary and secondary cells. Which types are used on motor vehicles?

Primary cells are non-reversible and therefore cannot be recharged.

Secondary cells are reversible and therefore can be recharged, and cells of this type are used on motor vehicles.

133. Motor vehicle batteries are almost always of the 'lead-acid' type. Why are they given this title?

Because the battery plates are made of lead and are immersed in an acid solution.

134. What is the difference between the positive and negative plates of a battery?

The spaces of the cast lead-alloy grid of the positive plate are filled with lead-peroxide paste, which has a dark-brown appearance in service. The spaces of the cast lead-alloy negative plate are filled with spongy lead paste, which is grey in color.

135. What is the function of a separator?

A separator is placed between each adjacent positive and negative battery plate in order to prevent the plates touching and therefore 'shorting.'

136. What material is used for battery separators?

Port Orford cedar, fibrous glass mat, porous rubber.

137. What are the constituents of electrolyte, and how is it made up?

Electrolyte is a dilute solution of sulphuric acid and distilled water. It is made up by adding (slowly) concentrated sulphuric acid to distilled water in the proportions of 1 part acid to between 2 to 4 parts of water to give the specific gravity required.

Safety Note: Never add water to acid — always add acid to water while constantly stirring solution.

138. What instrument should be used to determine the state of charge of a battery? What readings would indicate a fully charged, half-charged, and discharged battery?

A hydrometer. The following readings indicate the state of charge:

Fully charged:	1.275 to 1.285
Three-quarter charged:	1.250
Half-charged:	1.225
Discharged:	1.130

139. What effect has temperature on the specific gravity of battery electrolyte?

As the temperature rises, so the specific gravity readings of electrolyte fall and vice versa.

140. What will be the voltage of a single cell of a lead-acid battery in good condition, under the following conditions: (a) fully charged, (b) about half charged, and (c) discharged?

(a) Fully charged, about 2.5 volts, (b) about half charged, approximately 2.0 volts, (c) discharged, 1.8-1.9 volts.

141. When a battery is discharged both the negative and positive plates are covered with a film of lead sulphate, and the specific gravity of the electrolyte is low. What occurs when the battery is recharged?

The charging current converts the lead-sulphate film into active lead peroxide on the positive plates and active, spongy lead on the negative plates. The lead sulphate from the discharged plates combines with the electrolyte, strengthening it and raising the specific gravity.

142. What is 'sulphation' and briefly, what are its ill-effects?

When a discharged (or partly discharged) battery is allowed to stand unused for some time, the lead sulphate on the surface of the plates hardens. This prevents the battery charging or discharging properly.

143. Are any special frost precautions required for a battery?

None at all, provided the battery is kept in charged condition. Under conditions of severe frost, a discharged battery can freeze and crack the case.

144. How is battery capacity measured?

It is measured in ampere-hours, usually at the 10-hour rate. Thus, a battery of 60 ampere-hour capacity should, when fully charged, be able to discharge current at the rate of 6 amperes for 10 hours, after which it should be fully discharged.

145. What symptoms indicate that a battery is nearing the end of its useful life?

(a) Inability to hold its charge, (b) inability to turn the engine over briskly, (c) the ammeter (if fitted) showing a persistently high charging rate, (d) the lights becoming noticeably brighter when the engine is revved-up from idling, (e) flare-up.

Note: Symptoms (b) and (d) may also apply to a good battery: when part charged, or in cold weather, or when the battery terminals are loose or dirty.

146. What maintenance does a battery require?

(a) The electrolyte must be kept topped up with distilled water to about 1/8-in. above the level of the plates. (b) The terminals must be kept clean and tight. (c) The battery must be held firmly in position. (d) The top of the battery should always be wiped clean and dry. (e) The terminals and the fixing bolts can be prevented from corroding by smearing with petroleum jelly. (f) Lubriplate.

147. Using a heavy-discharge meter, what is the reading which would indicate that a battery was in good condition?

With the meter applied to each cell for 15 seconds the reading should be 1.5V to 1.8V per cell.

148. How can badly corroded battery terminals be cleaned?

(a) Wash with a warm solution of water and bicarbonate of soda and scrape clean. (b) Wash with ammonia solution.

149. What do the following terms mean in connection with batteries (generators-alternators)? (a) Electromotive force (e.m.f.); (b) Potential difference (p.d.); (c) Voltage drop (v.d.).

(a) This is the voltage across the terminals of a generator-alternator or battery when it is not supplying current to an outside circuit. (b) This is the voltage across the terminals of a alternator-generator or battery when it is under load. (c) This is the voltage loss which occurs when a alternator-generator or battery is put under load. It is the difference between the e.m.f. and the p.d.

150. The e.m.f. of a battery is 13.5V. When it supplies a current of 12 amperes to an outside circuit its p.d. is 11.5V. Find the v.d. of the battery and its internal resistance.

$$\text{v.d.} \qquad \text{v.d.} = \text{e.m.f.} - \text{p.d.}$$
$$= 13.5 - 11.5$$
$$= 2V$$

$$\text{Internal resistance} = \frac{\text{Voltage drop}}{\text{Amperes}}$$

$$R = \frac{E}{I} = \frac{2}{12}$$

$$= 0.165 \text{ ohm}$$

151. How is it possible to tell which terminal of a battery is negative and which is positive?

The positive terminal is the larger of the two and often marked with a +, the negative terminal marking being a minus sign −. In some instances the terminals may be colored: the positive red and the negative black.

THIRD YEAR

MOTOR VEHICLE TECHNOLOGY

LIMITS, FITS AND TOLERANCES

1. If the piston rings in an engine must be given a gap of 0.005 in. per inch of bore diameter, what will be the gap (to the nearest 0.001 in.) with a cylinder bore of 3.75-in. diameter?

$$\text{Gap size} = 0.005 \times 3.75$$
$$= 0.01875 \text{ in.}$$
To nearest 0.001 in. gap size = 0.019 in.

2. The standard size of a certain shaft is $2\frac{3}{16}$ in. diameter. In manufacture it will be accepted if it is not more than 0.0025 in. larger or 0.002 in. smaller than standard. What will be the diameter of the largest and smallest shaft permissible?

$2\frac{3}{16}$ in. = 2.1875 in.

Diameter of largest shaft = 2.1875 + 0.0025 = 2.19 in.
Diameter of smallest shaft = 2.1875 − 0.002 = 2.1855 in.

3. The dimensions of a shaft and its bearing are given below. Find the greatest and least possible running clearances that can exist between the shaft and bearing.

Shaft 1.997 ± 0.001 in., bearing 2.000 ± 0.0005 in.

Greatest clearance = largest bearing size − smallest shaft size
$$= 2.0005 \text{ in.} - 1.996 \text{ in.}$$
$$= 0.0045 \text{ in.}$$
Smallest clearance = smallest bearing size − largest shaft size
$$= 1.9995 \text{ in.} - 1.998 \text{ in.}$$
$$= 0.0015 \text{ in.}$$

4. In the previous question, what are the 'limits' to which the shaft may be made and what is the 'tolerance'?
   (a) Top limit size: Max. possible shaft diameter = 1.998 in.
       Bottom limit size: Min. possible shaft diameter = 1.996 in.
   (b) The tolerance is the margin of error between the maximum and minimum dimensions = 1.998 − 1.996 = 0.002 in.

5. (a) **What determines the class of fit between two mating parts?** (b) **Give one example of an drive fit and one of a clearance fit.**

(a) The 'allowance,' which is the difference in size of two mating parts. (b) Drive fit: valve guides in the cylinder-head. Clearance fit: king-pin in its bushes.

6. **Why is it that a component such as a connecting rod bearing must be made to very close tolerances?**

The fit of a component such as a connecting rod bearing, must be very precise, otherwise the engine will not work properly. Also when such parts are replaced by new ones, then the new parts must fit accurately.

CYLINDER BLOCKS, HEADS, GASKETS AND SLEEVES

7. **What are the principal materials from which cylinder blocks and cylinder-heads are made?**
Cast-iron or aluminum alloy.

8. **What are the advantages of using cast-iron cylinder blocks as opposed to aluminum alloy?**

(a) Good casting properties. (b) Free graphite helps to give good wearing properties. Cylinder bores, for example, can be machined directly in cast-iron. (c) Good sound-dampening properties. (d) Tapped holes (e.g. cylinder-head studs) less easily stripped than with aluminum.

9. **What are the advantages of aluminum cylinder blocks over those made from cast-iron?**

(a) Lighter in weight. (b) Attractive appearance. (c) Easier machining during production. (d) Better heat dissipation.

10. **What are four major comparative merits of cast-iron and aluminum alloy used in cylinder-heads?**

Cast-iron

(a) Good bearing surface for such things as valves running directly in cylinder-head.

(b) Valve seats can be made in parent metal of head.

(c) More difficult to machine during manufacture.

(d) Rate of heat dissipation is inferior to aluminum.

Aluminum Alloy

(a) Poor bearing material. Separate valve guides, etc., must be provided.

(b) Separate valve seat inserts of a harder material must be provided.

(c) Easy machining possible.

(d) Rate of heat dissipation is good.

11. **Name three types of cylinder-head gasket.**
(*a*) Copper/asbestos. (*b*) Solid copper. (*c*) Mild-steel 'shim' type.

12. **What is the usual order of tightening down cylinder-head studs, and what type of wrench should be used?**
Follow manufacturers specifications.

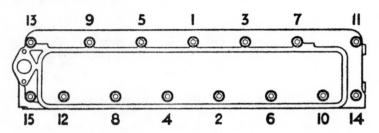

13. **What are the two types of cylinder sleeves?**
(*a*) Wet sleeves. (*b*) Dry sleeves.

14. **Explain the essential difference between the two types of cylinder sleeves.**
The outer surface of a wet sleeve is in direct contact with the cooling water. The outer surface of a dry sleeve is in contact with the inner wall of the engine cylinder.

15. **Some engine manufacturers fit dry cylinder sleeves as standard practice to brand-new engines. What are the advantages of this procedure?**
(*a*) Increased cylinder-bore life, as the sleeve can be made of an iron selected more for its wearing properties than its casting properties. (This may not be the case when casting the much more complicated shape of a cylinder block.) The more suitable wear-resisting materials do not cause an excessive rise in costs, as the volume of material required is small. (*b*) With slip-fit, pre-finished sleeves, when the cylinder bores become worn they can be easily renewed without any machining. (*c*) The sleeves can be made to have good corrosion resistance.

16. **What are the advantages of wet cylinder sleeves?**
(*a*) All the advantages given in parts (*a*) and (*c*) of the answer to the previous question. (*b*) They can be installed and removed easily without removing the engine from the chassis. (*c*) Wet sleeves are normally pre-finished, so that no boring or honing is needed after fitting. (*d*) Good, even cooling, as the sleeve is in direct contact with the cooling water. (*e*) Simpler cylinder-block casting, as no enclosed water-jacket is needed.

17. **What instruments may be used to determine the inside diameter of a cylinder bore?**

(*a*) An inside micrometer. (*b*) A dial gauge used in conjunction with cylinder measuring attachments. (Sometimes referred to as a cylinder, Starrett, or Mercer gauge.)

18. **Describe a method of determining the amount of wear in a cylinder, without the use of an inside micrometer.**

(*a*) Determine the original bore size. (*b*) Ascertain oversize (if any). (*c*) Set external micrometer to original bore size (plus oversize if any.) (*d*) Place foot of cylinder-measuring dial gauge between micrometer jaws and zero gauge. (*e*) Insert cylinder gauge into bore and rock gently back and forth to obtain minimum 'clock' reading. Any reading above zero, indicates the extent of wear at the point at which the gauge foot is positioned.

Note: Cylinder bore must, of course, be clean.

19. **Whereabouts in the engine is the combustion chamber?**

It is in the space which remains above the piston head when the piston reaches t.d.c.

Note: On some pistons, particularly in diesel engines, a large part of the combustion chamber may be formed of a hollowed-out portion of the piston head itself.

20. **What is the formula used to calculate the compression ratio of an engine?**

$$\text{Compression ratio} = \frac{\text{clearance volume} + \text{intake stroke volume}}{\text{clearance volume}}$$

21. **How can the face of a cylinder-head be checked for flatness?**

(*a*) Face to be checked must be thoroughly clean. (*b*) Place it on a large surface plate which has been smeared lightly with Prussian Blue. (*c*) Slide head gently back and forth several times. (*d*) Lift off head and observe face. 'Blued' spots indicate high spots.

Conversely where head has not picked blue indicates low spots.

Note: If head rocks when on surface plate, this indicates warp and can be checked by feeler gauges.

PISTONS AND RINGS

22. **Pistons are almost always made from one of three materials. What are these materials?**

(*a*) Cast iron. (*b*) Aluminum (alloy). (*c*) Cast steel.

23. Name the lettered parts of the piston.

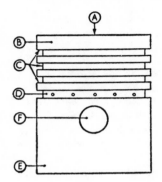

(A) Head. (B) Top land. (C) Compression ring grooves. (D) Oilscraper-ring groove. (E) Skirt. (F) Wrist pin hole.

24. What advantages have aluminum-alloy pistons over cast-iron pistons?

(a) Lighter in weight, allowing higher R.P.M. *(b)* Better thermal conductivity, allowing the use of higher compression ratios.

25. What advantages have cast-iron pistons over aluminum pistons?

(a) With a cast-iron piston running in a cast-iron block the expansion rate of both is very similar. Thus small running clearances can be given when the engine is cold, and these will be approximately maintained at engine-operating temperatures. *(b)* The wear rate of a cast-iron piston, particularly in a cast-iron block, is low due to the presence of free carbon in the cast iron. *(c)* The rate of wear of the ring grooves is low.

26. From what material would this piston be made, and what is the purpose of the vertical slot?

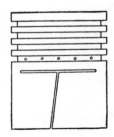

This would be an aluminum-alloy piston. With the slot, the skirt can expand without seizing in the cylinder bore, yet it still has only the minimum clearance when cold.

27. What is the purpose of the horizontal slot in the piston shown in the previous question?

It allows the skirt to expand circumferentially with the minimum of distortion and also forms a heat barrier. This directs the majority of the heat travelling from the head to the skirt, to the parts of the piston which have been designed with generous clearances.

28. Suggest two methods of preventing a fully floating wrist pin from scoring the cylinder walls.
(*a*) By a lock ring fitted in the wrist pin hole at both ends of the pin.
(*b*) By brass slippers on both ends of the wrist-pin.

29. To which side of the engine should the split skirt of an aluminum-alloy piston be fitted?
See manufacturers specifications for particular engine.

30. From what material are nearly all piston rings made?
Cast iron.

31. Sketch and name three types of piston-ring gap.

BUTT GAP   SCARF GAP   STEP GAP

32. What are the advantages of chrome-faced piston rings?
(*a*) Reduced cylinder bore wear. (*b*) Ring wear itself is less.

33. What particular precautions must be observed when fitting chrome rings?
(*a*) They must *never* be fitted into chromed bores. (*b*) Most chrome rings have 'top' marked on the upper side of the ring and the ring must be fitted facing the correct way.

34. Why is it that cast iron is almost universally used in the manufacture of piston rings?
(*a*) Good natural elasticity within the limits required. (*b*) Good resistance to high temperatures. (*c*) Easy to cast. (*d*) Excellent wearing properties.

35. What is the purpose of a gap in the piston ring?
(*a*) When manufactured, the ring has a slightly greater diameter than the cylinder bore. The gap allows it to be squeezed to fit into the bore, where it constantly exerts the necessary radial pressure on the cylinder walls. (*b*) To allow for expansion. (*c*) To enable the ring to be fitted on to the piston.

36. What are typical piston clearances for an aluminum-alloy piston?

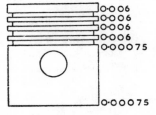

0·006
0·006
0·006
0·006
0·00075

0·00075

Clearances given in
thousandths of an inch
per inch of bore diameter.

All clearances should be measured at right angles to the wrist-pin axis.

37. What are typical piston clearances for a cast-iron piston?

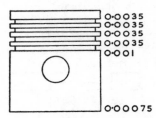

0·0035
0·0035
0·0035
0·0035
0·001

0·00075

Clearances given in
thousandths of an inch
per inch of bore diameter.

All clearances should be measured at right angles to the wrist-pin axis.

38. What are the recommended piston-ring gaps for *(a)* **air-cooled racing engines, and** *(b)* **all other engines?**
(a) 0.005 in. to 0.007 in. per inch of bore diameter; *(b)* 0.004 in. to 0.006 in. per inch of bore diameter.

39. What should be the side clearance of piston rings in their grooves?
Gasoline engines: 0.0015 in. to 0.0035 in.
Diesel engines: 0.0025 in. to 0.0045 in.
Air-cooled, two-stroke gasoline engines: 0.003 in. to 0.005 in.

40. How are pistons lubricated?
Usually by positive feed 'spit' hole or splash from connecting rod bearing.

CONNECTING RODS AND CRANKSHAFTS

41. How is a connecting rod normally made, and what metals are used for the rod and its bearings?

A connecting rod is normally a drop forging of steel with a bronze (or brass) wrist-pin end bushing and detachable white-metal connecting rod bearing shell bearings.

42. What other material is occasionally used for connecting rods?
Aluminum alloy.

43. State three advantages that aluminum alloy connecting rods have over steel connecting rods.

(a) Lighter in weight. *(b)* Wrist-pin end bearing need not be separate and can be bored directly into parent metal of rod. *(c)* Connecting rod bearing can be made as *(b)*.

44. If it is desired that the wrist-pin should not rotate in the connecting rod, how might it be fixed in position in the rod?

By means of a wrist-pin lock bolt.

45. What is a 'thin-wall' bearing?

This is a type of bearing most commonly employed for connecting rod bearing and main bearings. The soft bearing material is only a few thousandths of an inch in thickness on a curved steel shell, itself only about 1/16 in. thick.

46. The actual bearing material used to 'line' thin-wall bearings, varies according to the type of engine in which it is used. Suggest two typical examples.

(a) White metal Babbit, containing mainly tin, with small amounts of copper and antimony — used on small, light-duty gasoline engines. *(b)* Copper-lead, containing about one-third lead, the remainder being copper plus perhaps a very small percentage of tin — used in compression-ignition engines.

CYLINDER NUMBERS AND FIRING ORDERS

47. Engine cylinders are identified by giving them numbers. How is the numbering sequence arranged for an in-line engine?
This can vary according to the whim of the manufacturer.

48. How are cylinders numbered in the case of V or opposed cylinder engines?

Consult manufacturers specifications.

49. Give two alternative firing orders for both of the following in-lines engines: *(a)* **four cylinder, and** *(b)* **six cylinder.**

(a) 1342 or 1243. *(b)* 153624 or 142635.

50. If the six-cylinder shaft shown below was rotated clock-wise, what would be its firing order?

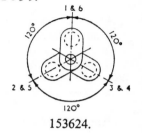

153624.

51. If the firing order of an engine is not known, by what simple practical method can it be determined?

By rotating the engine and watching the order in which the intake valves open.

Note: Present-day engines make it a difficult job to watch valve action without taking off a lot of covering. Simplest method would be to remove spark plugs and replace with corks. Turn engine over and watch sequence of cork popping. Or check manifolds for stamped firing order. Or check manufacturers specifications.

CRANKSHAFTS

52. Give two methods of manufacturing crankshafts, and state the metals used.

Most crankshafts are steel drop forgings. Some, however, are cast, using a specially developed cast iron.

53. Name the lettered parts of the crankshaft shown below.

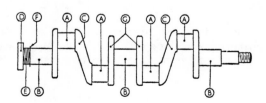

(A) Connecting rod bearing journals. (B) Main bearing journals. (C) Web. (D) Flywheel mounting flange. (E) Oil return thread. (F) Oil slinger ring. (G) Balance webs.

54. If a crankshaft for a four-cylinder engine was referred to as a 'five-bearing shaft,' what would this mean?
That the shaft had five main bearings, one on each side of every connecting rod bearing.

55. What is the maximum number of main bearings that you would expect to be fitted to a six-cylinder in-line engine?
Seven.

56. Give three advantages of having a main bearing on each side of every connecting rod bearing.
(a) Crankshaft is very stiff and well supported. (b) As a result of (a), engine is normally much smoother and long-lasting. (c) Because of the additional internal webs required to support the main bearings, the crankcase itself is much stiffer.

57. What are the two main disadvantages of the bearing arrangement as mentioned in the previous question.
(a) More expensive. (b) Engine may have to be slightly longer to accommodate the extra main bearings.

58. Name three types of oil retainers that could be fitted to a crankshaft to prevent oil leaking, say, in to clutch housing.
(a) Oil slinger ring and wind-back thread. (b) Lip-type seal. (c) Gland-type packing.

CRANKSHAFT LUBRICATION AND WEAR

59. How are crankshafts normally lubricated?
The shaft is pressure-fed from the main oil gallery with a supply to each main bearing. Internal drillings (or ducts) in the webs of the crankshaft conduct oil from the main bearings to each connecting rod bearing.

60. How much wear may take place on a crankshaft journal before it requires regrinding?
At approximately 0.003 in., regrinding is advisable. At 0.006 in., regrinding is essential.

61. A service manager has to decide whether to regrind or fit new bearings to a four-cylinder, three-bearing crankshaft. Lay out a suitable table in which to record the information he would need to know regarding the wear on the journals.

MAKE _ _ _ _ _ _ JOB NO. _ _ _ _ _ _			
BIG ENDS STD. SIZE _ _ UNDER SIZE _ _ _			
JOURNAL Nº	TAPER WEAR	OUT OF ROUND	MAX. WEAR
1			
2			
3			
4			
MAINS STD. SIZE _ _ _ UNDER SIZE _ _ _ _			
1			
2			
3			

OVERHEAD VALVE GEAR

62. Name three ways of operating overhead valves.
(a) By side-mounted camshaft, and push-rods and rockers. (b) By overhead camshaft and rockers. (c) By overhead camshaft operating directly on the valve stems (or tappets which fit over the valve stems).

63. Name two ways of conveying the drive from the crankshaft to an overhead camshaft.
(a) By means of chain drive (usually arranged in two stages). (b) By a train of gears.

64. State three reasons why overhead-valve engines are preferred as compared with side-valve engines.
(a) Improved accessibility during top-overhaul. (b) Higher compression ratios may be used. (c) Greater volumetric efficiency (better filling of cylinder).

65. At what speed does the camshaft rotate in relation to the crankshaft?
Half speed.

66. From what materials may valve-rockers be made?
(a) Cast-iron. (b) Pressed steel with hardened tips. (c) Drop forged steel for heavy-duty applications.

VALVES AND VALVE CLEARANCES

67. What is the name given to this type
of valve?

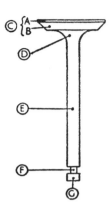

'Poppet' valve.

68. Name the lettered parts of this valve.
(A) Land. (B) Face. (C) Head. (D) Throat. (E) Stem. (F) Lock
groove. (G) Tappet.

69. What opens a valve and what closes it?
A valve is opened by its cam and closed by its spring.

**70. If the tappet clearances for an engine were given as 0.010
in. and 0.012 in., which setting would apply to which valves and
why?**
The intake valves would be given 0.010 in. clearance and the
exhaust valves 0.012 in. clearance. The exhaust valves run hotter
than the intake valves, expand more, and thus require the greater
clearance.

**71. When setting tappet clearances it is important to make
certain that the tappet is in its lowest position on the cam. Give
one method of doing this that could be used, for example, on a
five-cylinder engine.**
Rotate the engine until the tappet (or valve) to be set is fully
lifted, and then rotate the engine for one more complete revolution.
The tappet may now be set. Repeat this for the other valves.

**72. How is the actual operation of adjusting a tappet clearance
carried out on an ordinary o.h.v. engine?**

(i) The tappet must be in its lowest position as described in previous question. *(ii)* Test the clearance with the appropriate thickness of feeler gauge. *(iii)* Slacken off the lock-nut with a spanner and, with a screwdriver, turn the adjusting screw: clockwise to reduce the clearance; anti-clockwise to increase it. *(iv)* When the gap is correct, secure the lock-nut. *(v)* Recheck the gap after tightening the lock-nut.

Note: Most manufacturers recommend engine be running when adjusting valves.

73. Small seals are often fitted to only half the number of valves in an engine. To which valves are they fitted and why?

To the intake valves, in order to prevent oil being 'sucked' down the stem during the induction stoke and eventually being burned in the combustion chamber.

VALVE GUIDES

74. Name three materials that might be used for valve guides.

(a) Chilled cast-iron. *(b)* Phosphor bronze (usually inlets only). *(c)* Case-hardened mild-steel.

75. Many modern engines do not employ separate valve guides. What valve guide arrangement is then employed?

The valve stem runs directly in a hole (accurately reamed-out to size) in the parent metal of the cylinder-head. These are known as 'integral' guides.

76. An integral valve guide (as mentioned in the previous question) cannot be renewed. What procedure is adopted when it is worn?

The 'hole' is reamed-out oversize and a valve with an oversize stem is fitted.

77. Give three advantages of integral valve guides, as opposed to detachable guides.

(a) Cheaper. *(b)* Better cooling. *(c)* No possibility of becoming loose in service.

VALVE TIMING

78. What would be a typical valve-timing diagram for a medium-speed gasoline engine?

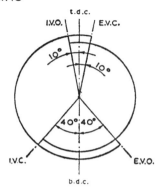

79. Referring to the diagram shown in the previous question, what are the valve-opening periods of: *(a)* the exhaust valve? *(b)* the intake valve?

(a) Exhaust valve-opening period 230°. *(b)* Intake valve-opening period 230°.

80. **What is meant by valve overlap and when does it occur?**

Valve overlap occurs when both the intake and exhaust valves of the same cylinder are open at the same time. It normally occurs about t.d.c. between the exhaust and intake strokes.

81. **What is meant by valve lead?**

This is when a valve opens before its stroke. It occurs if the exhaust valve opens during the power stroke before the exhaust stroke begins. It also occurs if the intake valve opens before the start of the intake stroke.

82. **What is meant by valve lag?**

This is when a valve remains open after its stroke has been completed. It occurs when the intake valve remains open after the piston has reached b.d.c. It also occurs when the exhaust valve does not close until after the piston has reached t.d.c.

83. **Why do the valves open and close at the points indicated in the answer to question 78 and not at the top and bottom dead centers?**

It has been found in practice that with the type of valve timing shown the filling and the scavenging of the cylinder is improved.

84. The intake valve on a certain high speed engine, opens 30°
before t.d.c. Calculate the distance from the t.d.c. mark measured
along the rim of the flywheel, at which the valve commences to
open (flywheel circumference = 48 in.).

$$\text{Distance from t.d.c. mark} = \text{circumference} \times \frac{\text{number of degrees}}{360}$$

$$= 48 \times \frac{30}{360}$$

$$= 4 \text{ in.}$$

LUBRICATION

85. **What is the purpose of lubrication?**
(a) To reduce wear. (b) To reduce friction. (c) To keep down the
temperature of moving parts and thus prevent seizure.

86. **What is the difference between a 'forced' and a 'fully forced'
engine lubrication system?**
With the fully forced system oil is delivered under pressure to
the wrist pin, and with the forced system it is not.

87. **Why is an oil-pressure relief valve essential?**
To maintain oil pressure at predetermined maximum pressure,
regardless of engine speed or temperature.

88. **Name the filter used on the intake side of the oil pump and
state the material from which it is made.**
The 'primary' filter, which consists of a fairly coarse wire gauze
surrounding the pump intake.

89. **Where in the engine lubrication system are 'secondary' filters
to be found and into what two types may they be divided?**
Secondary filters are always on the pressure side of the pump,
i.e. after the pump in the direction of oil flow, and are of either the
'full-flow' or the 'by-pass' type.

90. **Explain the difference between full-flow and by-pass filters.**
With a full-flow filter, all oil is filtered before it enters any of
the bearings. With a by-pass filter, only a small proportion of the
total oil flow passes through the filter, from which it is returned
to the sump.

91. What type of oil filter is illustrated here?

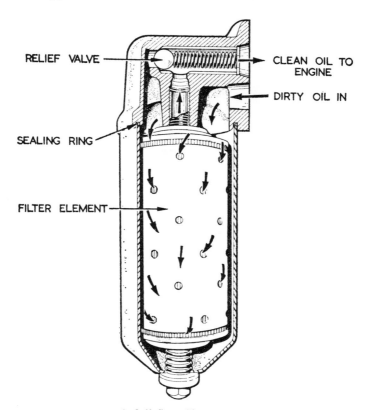

RELIEF VALVE

CLEAN OIL TO
ENGINE

DIRTY OIL IN

SEALING RING

FILTER ELEMENT

A full-flow filter.

92. **Some engine parts do not receive a supply of oil under pressure, but must rely on oil splash or mist for lubrication. Why is this?**

Such parts often cannot be pressure-fed in the same way as main bearings, etc. (e.g. timing chain) or it may be undesirable to feed them with large quantities of oil under pressure (e.g. intake valve stems). It has been found in practice that such parts can work well with splash and/or mist lubrication.

93. **Explain the difference between 'wet sump' and 'dry sump' lubrication systems.**

(a) With a 'wet sump' system the oil sump beneath the engine is the oil reservoir. Oil is pumped from there, around the engine, and returns there by gravity. *(b)* With a 'dry sump' system, a scavenge pump located in the sump returns the oil which would otherwise collect there, into a separate header tank. A separate pressure pump is used to supply oil from the header tank to the bearings.

94. Wet sump lubrication is almost universal on cars but where might dry sump lubrication be found?

Motor-cycles, some military and cross-country vehicles, and some high-performance sports and racing cars.

95. What are the advantages of a dry sump lubrication system?

(a) Without the need for a deep sump overall engine height can be reduced. *(b)* Oil reservoir can be at any convenient point on the vehicle and can be of any required capacity. *(c)* If reservoir is placed in air stream, it can act as an oil cooler. *(d)* It is possible, to use less oil (largely due to superior cooling) than with conventional sump. *(e)* If engine has to operate on severe gradients there is no chance of delivery pump being starved of oil.

96. Why is it important to change engine oil at the recommended intervals?

After the car has been in service for a period the oil becomes contaminated with carbon, sludge, gasoline, swarf, grit, and the like. Also, any additives the oil may contain can become exhausted, so that its lubrication properties become impaired and it must be renewed.

97. Give five possible causes of low oil pressure.

(a) Lack of oil in sump. *(b)* Oil too hot or too low viscosity. *(c)* Worn bearings. *(d)* Leaking oil pipe. *(e)* Primary filter partly blocked.

98. Many vehicles are fitted with an oil warning light instead of an oil-pressure gauge. What are the advantages and disadvantages of this practice?

Advantages: *(a)* Cheapness. *(b)* In the event of pressure failure the light should attract the driver's attention more quickly than would a gauge. *(c)* Simplicity, in that the oil pressure is either 'right' or 'wrong.'

Disadvantages: *(a)* Bulb failure renders the device inoperative. *(b)* It is not possible to observe the actual pressure in the system, which could be quite helpful in fault diagnosis.

99. How are ball and roller-bearings lubricated?

This depends largely upon their position on the vehicle, e.g. ball-bearings on a transmission cluster gear shaft may be submerged in oil, whilst wheel hub bearings are packed with grease on assembly. (These bearings are never lubricated by oil under pressure.)

100. Give an example of a self-lubricating bearing.

Some clutch release bearings are made of graphite, which is, in itself, a dry lubricant.

101. Give one example of a pre-lubricated bearing.

The phosphor bronze bushings carrying the starter-motor armature shaft are often impregnated with carbon during manufacture, and require no further lubrication during their life.

NOTE: *For further questions on lubrication and additives see Fourth Year Questions 137 to 153.*

GASOLINE AND COMBUSTION

102. What are the main constituents of normal gasoline and in what proportions do they occur?

Carbon: approx. 85 per cent by weight. *Hydrogen:* approx. 15 per cent by weight.

103. Does correct combustion produce an explosion inside the combustion chamber or merely a rapid burning?

A rapid burning.

104. State briefly what occurs during the combustion of a gasoline and air mixture.

The carbon from the gasoline and the oxygen from the air combine to burn and in so doing liberate heat to cause the rapid release of expanding gases inside the combustion space that will push the piston down on the power stroke.

Note: Various 'side-effects' occur, such as the production of water vapor, carbon monoxide, and carbon dioxide.

105. What will be the effect on the rate of combustion of (a) a slightly rich mixture and (b) a slightly weak mixture?

(a) Flame travel will become slower. (b) Flame travel will become faster, explosive mixture.

106. What would be the main effects on engine parts of using a very rich mixture?

(a) Some 'raw' gasoline would enter cylinder, wash away lubricant from cylinder walls, and get past piston to contaminate engine oil. (b) Heavy, sooty deposits would occur in the combustion chamber.

107. If an engine was running on an excessively weak mixture, what might be some of the main effects on engine parts?

(a) Overheating, particularly of such parts as valves, pistons and spark plugs. (b) Detonation and/or pre-ignition could occur as a result of (a).

EXHAUST GAS COMPOSITION

108. What is the normal composition of exhaust gas?

Nitrogen, carbon dioxide, some carbon monoxide, water, traces of methane, and perhaps hydrogen.

109. What will be the composition of exhaust gas when the engine is being fed with a weak mixture?

As in Question 108, but with less carbon dioxide, some free oxygen, and little or no carbon monoxide or hydrogen.

110. If the engine is receiving a rich mixture, what will be the composition of the exhaust gas?

As in Question 108, but with less carbon dioxide and more carbon monoxide.

DETONATION, PRE-IGNITION AND COMPRESSION RATIO

111. What is detonation?

It is an extremely rapid, explosive-like pressure rise inside the cylinder which occurs when some of the compressed mixture does not burn smoothly and progressively. It results in a greatly accelerated rate of combustion after the spark has occurred.

112. What is pre-ignition?

This occurs when the mixture is ignited by some source other than the ignition spark before the spark occurs.

Note: It can produce very similar results to detonation.

113. Give some of the main causes of detonation.

(a) Heavy carbon deposits in cylinders. *(b)* Ignition timing too far advanced. *(c)* Fuel being used is of too low octane value. *(d)* Engine overheated. *(e)* Feathered edge on valves.

114. What is meant by the octane number of fuel?

The octane number (or octane value) of a fuel is an indication of its tendency to detonate. The higher the octane number of a fuel, the greater its resistance to detonation.

115. If an engine has a high compression ratio, does it need fuel having a high octane value or a low octane value?

High octane value.

116. Why do high compression ratio engines demand high octane fuels?

Because of the higher pressures that occur in high compression engines which would cause low octane fuels to detonate.

117. Compression ratios are nowadays steadily being increased. What advantages result from this practice.

Both the power and the economy are directly improved by the increase in thermal efficiency, resulting from the higher compression ratios.

GASOLINE PUMPS

118. An A.C. mechanically operated fuel pump is shown here pictorially in section. State briefly how it works.

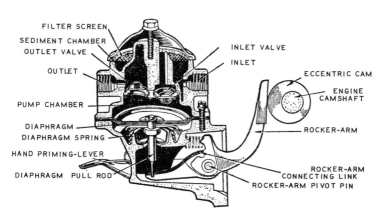

As the camshaft rotates, the eccentric forces against the rocker-arm and this, acting via the connecting link and diaphragm pull-rod, pulls the diaphragm downwards. This, in effect, increases the volume of the pump chamber causing therein a partial vaccum. The outlet valve is drawn on to its seat and the intake valve is drawn open. Atmospheric pressure acting on the surface of the fuel in the fuel tank, forces fuel along the pipe-line to fill up the partial vacuum in the pump chamber.

Further rotation of the camshaft, allows the eccentric (and rocker-arm) to move to the right. The diaphragm spring now forces the diaphragm upwards, pressurizing the fuel which closes the intake valve and opens to outlet valve allowing gasoline to flow to the carburetor.

119. How can a pump be tested to determine whether or not it is supplying fuel?

Remove (or slacken off) the delivery pipe union at the carburetor and rotate the engine a few times. The pump should deliver about half an egg-cupful of gasoline every two revolutions of the engine.

120. If an A.C. gasoline pump does not deliver fuel, what are the most likely causes?

(a) Lack of gasoline in the tank. (b) Loose filter bowl or damaged cork gasket. (c) Loose unions at the pump or tank. (d) Flexible gas line, from chassis pipe line to pump, drawing in air.

121. What other less common faults can cause a pump not to deliver gasoline?

(a) Faulty parts within the pump itself. (b) Blockage at the tank outlet. (c) Gasoline tank cap completely sealing tank. (Air must be able to enter the tank to allow the fuel to run out.) (d) Blocked pipe.

122. The illustration (see page 103) shows an S.U. fuel pump in section. What is its principal difference from the A.C. type pump?

Instead of the suction stroke of the diaphragm being caused by mechanical means, the diaphragm suction stroke is caused by electrical action. (See illustration on next page.)

123. What test will indicate whether or not an S.U. pump is delivering fuel?

Loosen off the carburetor supply union and, with the ignition switched on (engine stopped), fuel should gush out copiously.

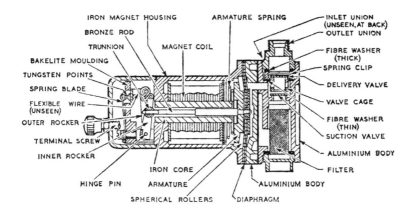

IRON MAGNET HOUSING   ARMATURE SPRING   INLET UNION (UNSEEN, AT BACK)
BRONZE ROD   OUTLET UNION
TRUNNION   MAGNET COIL   FIBRE WASHER (THICK)
BAKELITE MOULDING   SPRING CLIP
TUNGSTEN POINTS   DELIVERY VALVE
SPRING BLADE   VALVE CAGE
FLEXIBLE WIRE (UNSEEN)   FIBRE WASHER (THIN)
OUTER ROCKER   SUCTION VALVE
TERMINAL SCREW   ALUMINIUM BODY
INNER ROCKER   FILTER
IRON CORE
HINGE PIN   ARMATURE   ALUMINIUM BODY
SPHERICAL ROLLERS   DIAPHRAGM

124. What does a more-rapid-than-usual 'ticking' from an S.U. pump indicate?

(*a*) If it occurs when the ignition is first switched on after the car has been standing for some time, it is merely the pump working quickly to refill the carburetor. (*b*) Prolonged, very rapid, ticking, indicates that the pump is drawing in air, which is normally caused by lack of fuel in the tank or a leak on the suction side of the pump. (*c*) It could mean that fuel was leaking out beyond the pump.

125. If an S.U. pump fails to tick when the ignition is switched on, what might be the cause?

(*a*) The carburetor is full and does not require any more fuel. (*b*) The contact-breaker point faces are dirty or burnt out. (*c*) There is no supply of current to the pump. (*d*) There is a fault within the pump itself.

CARBURATION

126. What is the mixture characteristic of a simple jet?
Mixture goes progressively richer with increasing speed.

127. What is the mixture characteristic of a gravity, or submerged, jet?
Mixture goes progressively weaker with increasing speed.

128. What is meant by the terms 'fixed choke' and 'variable choke' as applied to carburetors?

(a) Fixed choke — this is where the venturi (i.e. choke) is of a fixed size and does not alter during the running of the engine. Examples of this are Zenith and Solex carburetors.

(b) Variable choke — this is where the carburetor throat (equivalent to the venturi or choke) constantly varies in size according to an engine's air/fuel requirements during the running of the engine. Examples include S.U. and Stromberg H.D. carburetors.

129. What is the difference between a constant-pressure and variable-pressure type of carburetor?

In a constant-pressure carburetor the air speed and depression over the jet does not vary, e.g. as in the S.U. carburetor. In a variable-pressure carburetor the air speed, and therefore depression over the jet, varies according to engine speed, e.g. as in Solex and Zenith carburetors.

130. By what method is mixture compensation achieved in Zenith carburetors?

By incorporating a gravity jet and a simple jet in the same carburetor. Thus the weakening characteristic of the former is balanced by the richening characteristic of the latter, and a constant mixture strength can be obtained over the speed range.

131. By what method is mixture compensation achieved by S.U. carburetors?

By means of a constant vacuum over the jet and varying the effective size of the jet. Sometimes referred to as the 'variable-choke' type.

132. By what method is mixture compensation achieved by Solex carburetors?

By the 'air-bleed' principle.

133. What form of acceleration device is used on S.U. carburetors?

An hydraulic damper is incorporated in the piston rod. This has the effect of slowing down any sudden rise of the piston. When the throttle valve is opened wider the extra air entering the engine must as a result pass through the choke opening, which is temporarily too small, at a higher velocity than usual. This causes a higher vacuum than normal over the jet, and draws a rich accelerating mixture into the engine.

134. Name two types of acceleration device commonly found on fixed-choke carburetors.

(a) Simple plunger pump, coupled to accelerator linkage so that if accelerator is depressed quickly, pump supplies an extra supply of gasoline into the air stream.

(b) A spring-operated diaphragm pump. The diaphragm is held back against the spring by the vacuum in the induction manifold. Suddenly opening the throttle lowers the vacuum and the spring then forces the diaphragm forward so as to discharge extra fuel into the air stream.

135. How may a rich mixture for starting be obtained on a Zenith carburetor?

A choke valve, fitted on the air-inlet side of the carburetor throat is closed. As a result, only a small amount of air can enter the engine, and this, in combination with fuel drawn from the main system, produces a rich mixture.

136. What arrangement is commonly employed on Solex carburetors to supply a rich starting mixture?

The throttle butterfly valve is closed, and gasoline and air in pre-determined proportions are fed to the engine by outlets below the throttle. This mixture is supplied by what is, in effect, a separate starting carburetor, on the side of the main carburetor and sharing the same float chamber.

137. State the proportion of air to gasoline in a chemically correct mixture.

(a) 15 parts of air to 1 part of gasoline (by weight). (b) 12.5 parts of air to 1 part gasoline (actual).

138. State the approximate proportions of air to gasoline (by weight) suitable for the following conditions: (a) starting; (b) idling; (c) acceleration; (d) economy; (e) full power.

(a) Starting, 9:1; (b) idling, 12:1; (c) acceleration, 12:1; (d) economy, 16:1; (e) full power, 12:1.

139. Why is the carburetor designed to supply a rich mixture when starting an engine from cold?

Only a portion of the fuel (known as the lighter ends of fractions) will vaporize at starting temperatures. To ensure a sufficient proportion of these lighter fractions, a rich mixture is supplied by the carburetor. The ratio of gasoline vapor to air entering the cylinders is, however (very approximately), of chemically correct proportions.

140. Why is it that a rich mixture is needed during idling?

At idling speeds exhaust-gas scavenging is poor, and consequently the new charge is contaminated by the presence of unexpelled burnt gases. Also the low gas velocity in the manifold causes some condensation of the heavier fractions of the fuel within the manifold.

141. Why is it most important with an S.U. carburetor to make sure that the fuel-air-ratio setting at idling speed is correct?

Any discrepancy in mixture strength at idling speed will be present throughout the whole of the speed range. Thus, for example, if the idling mixture were set slightly rich, then a slightly rich mixture would be delivered at all speeds.

COOLING SYSTEMS

142. What are the two types of cooling systems?

Liquid-cooling and air-cooling. Liquid-cooling is uniform throughout engine, and prevents hot spots.

143. What are the advantages of liquid-cooling?

(a) It is generally considered more suitable than air-cooling for multi-cylinder engines. (b) Water has a very high specific heat (a small amount of water is able to absorb a large amount of heat.) (c) Water is cheap and easily obtainable. (d) By means of a thermostat, engine temperature can be controlled. (e) Engine noise is reduced by having to pass through the water-jacket. (f) Engine-heated water can be used to heat the car interior, and in some cases the intake manifold.

144. What are the disadvantages of liquid-cooling?

(a) Water freezes and in cold weather may cause damage due to freezing. (b) Loss of cooling water may cause the engine to run hot and, in an extreme case, seize up. (c) Generally more expensive than air-cooling. (d) The presence of the water, radiator, pump, etc., makes the system heavy and bulky. (e) Takes power from the engine to operate pump and fan.

145. What are the advantages of air-cooling?

(a) Cheaper to manufacture, both in labor and materials. (b) Will not freeze up. (c) Cylinder and cylinder head-castings are less complicated, as water-jacketing is not required. (d) Engine weight is reduced. (e) Bulk may be reduced, as no radiator is required. (f) Engine warms up more quickly.

146. What are the disadvantages of air-cooling?

(a) Not suitable for multi-cylinder engines, unless a fan (which absorbs power) is used. (b) Greater mechanical noise, particularly if a fan is used. (c) Interior heating of car is generally not as satisfactory as with liquid system. (d) Develops hot spots.

147. Pump-assisted liquid-cooling systems are virtually universal on motor vehicles. What are the advantages of the system?

(a) Cooled liquid may be directed to places where it is most required, e.g. valve seats and spark-plug bosses.

(b) Particularly useful to ensure adequate circulation with o.h.v. engines, where liquid passages in the cylinder-head may be small.

(c) Smaller radiator required, therefore less liquid, and consequently less weight.

(d) Radiator may be in almost any desired position, thus giving more scope to body designer.

(e) Liquid circulation is positive and increases as engine r.p.m. increases.

(f) Liquid will circulate easily through an interior heater.

(g) System may be pressurized.

148. The boiling point of the liquid in a cooling system is often raised above 100°C or 212°F. How is it done?

By pressurizing the system.

149. To approximately what extent is a cooling system pressurized?

Usually about 4 lb psi to 7 lb psi. However, some systems, notably on American cars and W.D. vehicles, may go up as high as 10 lb psi to 15 lb psi on air conditionned vehicles.

150. By approximately how much is the boiling point of liquid raised when its pressure is increased by 1 lb psi, and what are the advantages of pressure cooling?

(a) 1 lb psi rise in pressure raises the boiling point by approximately 2½°F.

(b) With the cooling system pressurized, the boiling point of the coolant is raised, and thus the engine can be run hotter, giving greater thermal efficiency.

(c) No loss of coolant due to evaporation, since overflow is sealed, except when too great a pressure builds up and lifts pressure-release valve off its seat. Therefore less topping-up necessary.

(d) No loss of coolant due to surge.

(e) Radiator temperature is higher, so the radiator dissipates more heat. Consequently the size, weight, and cost of radiator are reduced.

(f) Because of (e), less liquid is required, so the vehicle is lighter and requires less anti-freeze.

(g) The pressure in the system is kept constant and this helps to avoid boiling troubles on high-altitude roads.

(h) Scale deposits are slow to form.

151. What would be the layout and appearance of a simple type radiator?

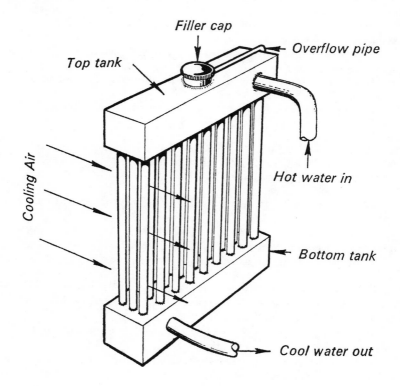

Filler cap

Overflow pipe

Top tank

Cooling Air

Hot water in

Bottom tank

Cool water out

152. Make simple line diagrams of two types of radiator construction.

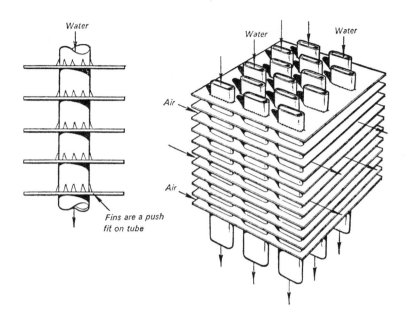

153. What are the advantages of a sealed cooling system?

(a) If it is leak-free, it will never need topping up. (b) Internal corrosion of the cooling system is very greatly reduced. (c) Anti-freeze solution may be kept in use for extended periods.

154. From what ill-effects can an engine suffer when it is over-cooled?

(a) Increased cylinder wear. (b) Dilution of oil due to poor vaporization of gasoline. (c) Greater formation of sludge. (d) Oil does not thin out properly and fluid friction losses are increased. (e) Engine will not achieve full power. (f) Burnt gases which leak past piston condense in crankcase to form corrosive acids in oil. (g) Lower thermal efficiency (less m.p.g.).

155. What may be the ill-effects of under-cooling an engine?

(a) Detonation and/or pre-ignition. (b) Possible seizure in bad cases. (c) More rapid coolant evaporation or, in an extreme case, liquid may boil. (d) Oil may become very thin, possibly causing heavy oil consumption and leakage. *(e)* Oil film may be burnt away. *(f)* Density of charge entering cylinder may become less if ingoing charge receives too much heat.

156. What is the function of a thermostat and where is it located?

It is a temperature-sensitive valve, usually fitted in its own housing on the cylinder-head, and is accessible when the top hose (and/or the thermostat housing) is removed. It enables the engine to warm up quickly by restricting the liquid flow to the radiator until the engine has achieved its operating temperature.

157. What are the two main types of thermostats in general use?

(a) Alcohol bellows type. *(b)* Bi-metallic spring (properly known as "wax jacks").

158. Bi-metallic spring thermostats are rapidly displacing the alcohol bellows type thermostats. What are their advantages?

(a) They are relatively insensitive to variations of pressure in the cooling system.

(b) Not having bellows which are constantly flexing, the bi-metallic spring thermostats do not suffer from metal fatigue in the same way as do the bellows type.

(c) Opening and closing temperatures can be very accurately controlled (largely as a result of *(a)*).

159. What are the disadvantages of the bi-metallic spring type thermostat compared with the bellows type?

(a) Slightly more expensive.

(b) They do not "fail-safe." If a failure occurs the valve remains closed, whereas with failure of the bellows type the valve remains open.

CLUTCH

(See Second Year Questions 23 to 25.)

160. What is the basic material of which most clutch-linings are made and what is the approximate coefficient of friction between the lining and the pressure plate or flywheel?

The basic material of most clutch-linings is asbestos, bonded with resin.

The coefficient of friction varies with the type of bonding material used from about 0.3 to about 0.5.

161. **What are three main advantages of a diaphragm spring clutch, over a conventional type clutch?**

(a) Fewer parts. (b) Lighter pedal loads needed. (c) Lighter in weight.

162. **What is the purpose of a spring center in a clutch disc?**

To dampen out torsional vibration in the transmission.

163. **What is the effect of no free travel at the clutch pedal?**

The clutch-release bearing will be pushing against the release levers, and thus the tendency will be to release the clutch. This could result in clutch slip and undue wear of the release mechanism and linings.

164. **What is the effect of too much free travel at the clutch pedal?**

The clutch may not free properly even with the clutch pedal fully depressed, thus causing clutch drag.

165. **Define "clutch slip."**

This occurs when the clutch does not transmit the full amount of engine torque being produced.

166. **Define "clutch drag."**

This occurs if the clutch is not completely released when the clutch pedal is fully depressed. As a result, some torque is always being transmitted by the clutch.

167. **Give three reasons for clutch slip.**

(a) Oil or grease on linings. (b) Lack of requisite free play at pedal. (c) Worn driven-plate linings.

168. **Give three reasons for clutch drag.**

(a) Oil or grease on linings. (b) Incorrect pedal adjustment, not allowing full movement of release bearing. (c) Driven-plate hub seized on splines.

169. **What is clutch chatter?**

This is when the whole car chatters (or shudders) when the drive is being taken up.

170. **How can clutch chatter be cured?**

Some models are slightly susceptible to it even when new and in these cases often very little can be done. Where chatter suddenly, or progressively, appears with a previously trouble-free vehicle, it is usually caused by one or more of the following: (a) loose, broken or sloppy engine mountings; (b) loose or broken engine stabilizer bars, rods, or cables; (c) oil or grease on the clutch linings; (d) Weak pressure plate springs; (e) Cracked or glazed pressure plate.

171. What is the formula used to determine the torque transmitted by a friction clutch?

Torque transmitted = total spring force × coefficient of friction × mean radius of linings × number of pairs of friction faces.

172. What formula could be used to determine the horse-power transmitted by a clutch?

$$\text{h.p.} = \frac{2\pi NT}{33000} \text{ where } \begin{aligned} N &= \text{R.P.M.} \\ T &= \text{torque in ft. lb.} \end{aligned}$$

GEARBOXES

(See Second Year Questions 26 to 29.)

173. What are the advantages of synchromesh gearboxes as opposed to sliding-mesh-type gearboxes?

(a) Smoother, easier gear-changing, with less wear and tear on transmission.

(b) Less skill in gear-changing required.

(c) As all the gears are in constant mesh, they can be made of helical, or double-helical, pattern. Therefore, they are stronger and quieter than the usual straight-cut gears used in a sliding-mesh gearbox.

174. What are the disadvantages of synchromesh gearboxes as compared with sliding-mesh type gearboxes?

(a) More expensive.

(b) When synchromesh cones wear, their synchronizing effect is reduced.

(c) It is sometimes possible to "beat" the synchromesh by very rapid gear-changing (virtually impossible on modern perfected designs).

(d) Design is much more complicated.

175. **If an idler gear is interposed between two gears, what effect does it have on:** (a) **the direction of rotation of the output gear?** (b) **the gear ratio of the two gears?**

(a) The output shaft is made to rotate in the opposite direction to its previous rotation, i.e. it now turns in the same direction as the input gear.

(b) It has no effect on the gear ratio.

176. **What does a gear-locking device usually consist of and why is it used?**

It usually consists of a spring-loaded steel ball, operating in notches on the gear-selector shaft. Its purpose is to hold the selector fork (and gear) in any desired gear or neutral position.

177. **For what purpose is a gear-interlocking device used?**

So as to allow only one gear to be engaged at a time.

178. **How are the various parts of an ordinary gearbox lubricated?**

Approximately the lower third of the box is filled with oil which splashes about inside the box when the vehicle is in use.

179. **When calculating gear ratios (velocity or speed ratios) it is necessary to know which one of a pair of gears is the driver and which one is the driven. In the following pairs of gears which is the driver gear?**

(a) Main drive pinion and cluster gear.
(b) First sliding gear and cluster gear.
(c) Master gear and pinion.

(a) Main drive pinion. (b) Cluster gear first speed. (c) Pinion.

180. **What are the two formulae used to calculate the gear ratio of a gearbox?**

(a) $\dfrac{\text{Number of teeth on driven}}{\text{Number of teeth on driver}} = \text{Gear ratio}$

(b) $\dfrac{\text{Speed of driver}}{\text{Speed of driven}} = \text{Gear ratio}$

SUSPENSION AND STEERING

181. **What type of springing is normally employed with beam axles?**

Semi-elliptic leaf springs.

182. What is meant by the term "independent suspension"?

Each wheel is separately sprung, and spring movement on one wheel does not necessarily affect any other wheel, as it would with a beam axle.

183. What are the advantages of independent front suspension?

(a) The wheels on deflection are not excessively tilted, and as they are not connected by a beam, wobble due to gyroscopic action is almost negligible.

(b) Elimination of wobble allows a greater deflection of the front wheels. Thus front springs are softer than rear springs, and body pitching (fore and aft) is reduced.

(c) Unsprung weight is reduced. This reduces the tendency of the tires to leave the road on rough surfaces and so improves road-holding.

(d) Better cornering.

(e) Improved passenger comfort.

184. What are the disadvantages of independent front suspension?

(a) Increased tire wear. (b) More expensive than beam axle layout. (c) More wearing parts requiring more maintenance. (d) The quality of the ride depends very greatly on the shock-absorbers. (e) Special equipment is required to check steering angles accurately.

185. Before checking any steering angles or measurement what other points must first be checked?

(a) Vehicle to be checked should be on firm, level ground. (b) Tires should be inflated to their correct pressures. (c) The vehicle should be laden, if necessary, to the amount specified by the makers. (d) The wheels must not be buckled, maximum runout allowable 1/8 in. (e) Wheel bearings, steering joints, shackle-pins, suspension pivots, and the like must be in good order.

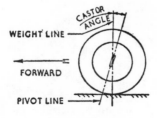

186. With the aid of a sketch, explain how castor action can be obtained, and show the position of the castor angle.

Castor action occurs when the pivot line strikes the ground ahead of the weight at ground level.

187. **What is the object of castor action?**

To provide self-centering action for the steering. The wheel then tends to return to the straight-ahead position after it has been deflected from its straight-ahead path.

188. **With the aid of a sketch, explain wheel camber, and show the position of the camber angle.**

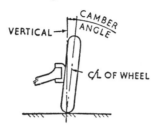

Camber is the amount by which the road wheel is tilted out of the vertical. It is expressed in degrees.

189. **What are positive and negative camber?**

Positive camber is when the wheels are tilted as shown in the answer to Question 188. That is, they are nearer together at the bottom than at the top.

Negative camber is when the wheels are tilted so that they are closer together at the top than at the bottom.

190. **What is the object of cambering the front wheels?**

To obtain, or help to obtain, center-point (or approximately center-point) steering, which, briefly, improves the lightness of the steering.

191. **With the aid of a sketch, explain king-pin inclination (king-pin cant) and show the angle of king-pin inclination.**

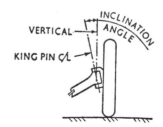

King-pin inclination is the amount in degrees that the king-pin is tilted out of the vertical, its lower end pointing towards the road wheel.

192. What is the object of inclining the king-pin as shown in the answer to Question 191?

To obtain, or help to obtain, center-point (or approximately center-point) steering.

193. Suggest one reason why it is necessary to "toe-in" the front wheels?

Wheels which are cambered (positive camber) tend to roll outward. By toeing-in the wheels this action is counteracted and the wheels will roll forward in a true path.

194. Briefly define the "Ackerman" steering layout.

With the wheels pointing straight ahead, a line drawn through the center of one king-pin and through the center of its adjacent steering knuckle arm ball joint, shall intersect a corresponding line drawn through the other king-pin and steering knuckle arm ball joint, at (or about) the center of the rear axle.

BRAKES

195. What are the essential features of a typical drum brake assembly?

See diagram below.

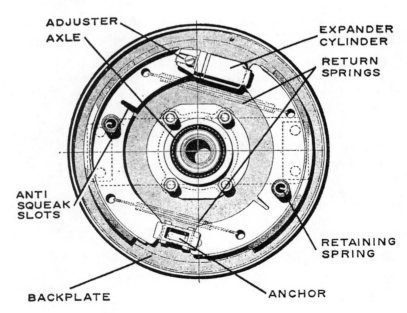

196. What are the essential features of a disc brake?
See diagram below.

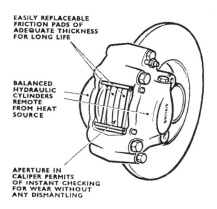

EASILY REPLACEABLE
FRICTION PADS OF
ADEQUATE THICKNESS
FOR LONG LIFE

BALANCED
HYDRAULIC
CYLINDERS
REMOTE
FROM HEAT
SOURCE

APERTURE IN
CALIPER PERMITS
OF INSTANT CHECKING
FOR WEAR WITHOUT
ANY DISMANTLING

197. What are the advantages of disc brakes?
(a) They are virtually fade-free, even under the most arduous conditions. (b) Adjustment for pad wear is automatic. (c) The state of pad wear can be checked without dismantling. (d) Pad renewal can normally be done quickly and easily.

198. What are the disadvantages of disc brakes?
(a) Slightly higher pedal pressures may be required if the car is not equipped with servo assistance. (b) Rate of pad wear is greater than would be expected on linings of similar-capacity drum brakes. (c) When disc brakes are fitted to the rear axle, the handbrake mechanism is often not particularly effective.

199. Why is the presence of air undesirable in a hydraulic system?
The effectiveness of a hydraulic braking system depends on the fact that the fluid used is virtually incompressible. Thus the pressure created when the master-cylinder piston is pushed forward is transmitted with practically no loss through the fluid in the pipelines to the wheel cylinders. If air is present in the system some, or all, of the brake pedal travel is used up in compressing that air. Therefore, there is a loss of braking effort.

200. If the brake pedal in a hydraulic braking system had to be pushed well down before the brakes started to act, what might the trouble be?

(a) Clearance between shoes and drum too great. Brakes require adjusting. *(b)* Pedal free play excessive. *(c)* Air in system, brakes require bleeding.

201. Describe how to bleed a hydraulic braking system.

(a) Fill supply tank with correct type of fluid and keep it filled throughout the operation.

(b) Attach a rubber tube to the bleeder nipple on one wheel cylinder. Allow the free end of the tube to hand into a clean glass jar containing sufficient fluid to cover the end of the tube.

(c) Release bleeder nipple by about one turn.

(d) "Pump" the brake pedal by depressing it slowly to the full extent of its travel and allowing it to return unassisted. Allow a slight pause between each downward stroke. Watch the flow of fluid into the glass jar, and when all air bubbles cease to appear tighten bleeder screw while pedal is held in the down position.

(e) Repeat the foregoing at all the remaining wheel cylinders.

202. What would cause unbalanced braking with hydraulic brakes?

(a) Oil or grease on linings. *(b)* Tires unevenly inflated. *(c)* Tires in different states of wear. *(d)* Loose steering connections. *(e)* Vehicle fitted with linings having varying coefficients of friction. *(f)* Loose brake back plate (or disc). *(g)* Broken or loose springs. *(h)* Distorted brake drums (or discs).

203. What is the approximate coefficient of friction which normally exists between the brake linings and the drum or disc and pad?

In the region of 0.3 to 0.5.

204. What may cause the coefficient of friction between a brake lining and drum to vary?

(a) Oil or grease on lining. *(b)* Water on lining. *(c)* Brakes overheated.

205. What are the main factors affecting the braking effort?

(a) The coefficient of friction between the tire and the road. *(b)* The coefficient of friction between the braking surfaces. *(c)* The force applied to the pedal. *(d)* The type of braking system employed.

206. If a vehicle was said to have brakes with an efficiency of 100 per cent, or 1.0g, what would these expressions mean?

If a vehicle can be braked with a retarding force equal to the weight of that vehicle, it decelerates at the rate of acceleration due to gravity or 32 ft/s^2. This is a braking efficiency of 100 per cent or 1g.

207. By what methods can the efficiency of a braking system be measured?

(a) By measuring the stopping distance. (b) By measuring the time required to stop. (c) By use of a decelerometer. (d) By use of a brake-testing machine.

208. Which are considered to be the best methods of testing braking efficiency?

The use of either a decelerometer or a brake-testing machine.

209. Does the stopping distance of a vehicle increase at the same rate as the increase in speed?

No. Stopping distances increase as the square of the increase in speed. For instance, if a vehicle which stops in 16 ft. from 20 m.p.h. doubles its speed, its stopping distance will increase $2^2 (= 4)$ times, to 64 ft. If its speed is trebled to 60 m.p.h., its stopping distance will increase $3^2 (= 9)$ times, to 144 ft.

210. What would be the stopping distance (in feet) from 30 m.p.h. with brakes of the following efficiencies:

(a) 30 per cent or 0.3g. (b) 40 per cent or 0.4g. (c) 50 per cent or 0.5g. (d) 70 per cent or 0.7g. (e) 100 per cent or 1.0g.

	Efficiency	Stopping Distance in Feet
(a)	30 per cent or 0.3g.	100
(b)	40 per cent or 0.4g.	75
(c)	50 per cent or 0.5g.	60
(d)	70 per cent or 0.7g.	43
(e)	100 per cent or 1.0g.	30

211. What is brake fade?

When the effectiveness of the brakes is reduced by an excessive build-up of heat at the brake-drums. In an extreme case, even the hardest pedal pressure will produce little or no retarding effect.

WHEELS AND TIRES

212. Road wheel sizes on modern cars have gradually tended to become smaller. What are the advantages of smaller wheels?

(a) Reduced unsprung weight, giving better road-holding.

(b) Lower initial cost.

(c) Wheel arches intrude less into passenger space.

(d) Smaller wheels lower the height of the car and its center of gravity.

(e) Maximum steering-lock angles can usually be increased as smaller wheels require less space when on lock.

(f) Spare wheel requires less storage space.

213. What type of construction is used for most wheels today?
Most present-day wheels are of pressed-steel construction.

214. Spoked wheels are becoming more popular with some types of cars. What are their advantages over pressed-steel wheels?
(a) Sporty appearance. (b) Better air flow around brakes. (c) Spoked wheels are slightly springy.

215. What are the disadvantages of spoked wheels?
(a) More expensive. (b) Difficult to keep clean. (c) Tubeless tires cannot be used on them. (d) Spokes can tend to work loose in service.

216. What are the advantages of tubeless tires over the conventional tire and tube?
(a) Air pressure is maintained for a much longer period. (b) Loss of air due to nail-type punctures is virtually eliminated. (c) Slightly more resistant to impact blows. (d) No possibility of pinching the tube when fitting. (e) Ordinary punctures are easy to repair, and in some cases can be repaired without removing the tire from the wheel. (f) Heat, due to friction between tube and tire casing is eliminated.

217. What are the disadvantages of tubeless tires compared to the conventional tire and tube?
(a) Unsuitable for spoked wheels. (b) Unsuitable for damaged or corroded wheels. (c) Tubeless tires are stiffer and give a slightly firmer ride.

218. What special points should be noted when fitting tubeless tires?
(a) Rim flanges must be smooth and clean. (b) Care must be taken not to injure the bead. (c) Before inflating apply a tourniquet round the circumference of the tire and spring the beads on to the rim. (d) After inflating, test for leaks by submerging the tire and wheel in water.

219. What are "radial ply" tires?
These are tires in which the plies (i.e. layers of fabric) do not cross one another at an angle, but the threads of the plies are all

positioned radially from the center of the wheel and form a continuous series of "hoops" from one bead to the other.

220. What are the advantages of "braced tread" tires over conventional tires?

(a) Improve cornering ability. (b) Less tread "shuffle" on the road, which results in increased tread life and slightly improved fuel consumption.

221. Mention three very important characteristics of modern-type tread design.

(a) The use of high-mu rubber which has excellent road-grip qualities.

(b) Longitudinal channels to convey bulk of rain-water away from contact area as rapidly as possible.

(c) The "multi-snipe" concept, where thousands of fine "knife-cuts" help to disperse the final layer of water from the road surface in order that at least part of the contact area can obtain a dry grip.

222. What are the chief factors affecting tire life?

(a) Inflation pressure. (b) Speed and rate of acceleration. (c) Wheel alignment and steering geometry. (d) Brakes. (e) Road conditions. (f) Temperature. (g) Tire rotation. (h) Tire and wheel balance.

223. Why does under-inflation reduce tire life?

Excessive distortion of tire walls results in their cracking and in cord breakage. Heat generated from friction between cord layers inside tire helps the breakdown to occur.

224. What adverse effects, other than that of reduced tire life, may result from under-inflation?

(a) Lack of directional stability of the vehicle. (b) Increased rolling resistance and therefore increased fuel consumption. (c) Tread wear is uneven. (d) In a severe case a tire may creep on its rim and with a conventional tube may rip the valve out.

225. What are the results of over-inflation?

(a) Tire cushioning properties are reduced. (b) Greater chance of fracture and cutting, as casing and tread are subject to greater tension. Impact resistance is reduced. (c) Tread wear is confined to a smaller section of tread. (d) Road-holding properties are reduced.

226. For what reason does tread wear increase with speed?

(a) Operating temperature is increased, because of more deflections per minute. The resistance of the tread rubber to abrasive wear decreases as temperature rises. (b) Acceleration and braking tends to be more fierce. (c) Tire slip and distortion when rounding bends and corners is increased. (d) Minor road irregularities produce more bounce and scuffing wear than would be the case at low speeds.

227. What symptoms would lead you to believe that the wheels of a car required balancing?

(a) A vibration, often felt through the steering wheel, occurring at certain critical road speeds. (b) Uneven tire wear.

228. Wheels are balanced statically and dynamically. Briefly, what do these terms mean?

(a) Static balance is balance in a single plane. When a wheel is allowed to spin freely there will be no tendency for any particular part of the wheel to come to rest at the lowest point.

(b) Dynamic balance is balance in two (or more) planes. This is to correct the tendency of the wheel to oscillate about its center.

229. Make a sketch to show the points from which tire section width, height, and overall diameter, and wheel diameter are measured.

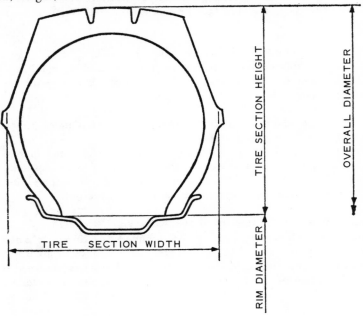

230. Is the size of the tire section width equal to the tire section height?

With the older "super balloon" tires they were approximately equal; the height being 95 per cent of the width (European Standard). With modern tires, the section width tends to be considerably greater than the height.

231. What are low section tires?

These are tires whose section height is 88 per cent of the width (European Standard).

232. What are ultra-low profile tires?

These are tires whose section height is 80 per cent (or less) of the width.

See Fourth Year Questions 81 to 84 for problems dealing with slip angle, understeer and oversteer.

CALCULATIONS, SCIENCE AND LABORATORY WORK

ENGINE TESTING

See Fourth Year Questions 190 to 206.

STRESS AND STRAIN

For problems dealing with stress and strain see Second Year Questions 69 to 81.

SPRING TESTING

233. What is the rate, or stiffness, of a spring?

The rate of a spring is measured in pounds per inch and is the force required to compress (or extend) the spring by 1 inch.

$$\text{Rate} = \frac{\text{load}}{\text{deflection}}$$

234. Is the answer to Question 233 correct for leaf, torsion bar, and helical springs?

Yes. Spring rate is found in the same manner for both leaf and helical springs.

235. Is the rate of any given spring constant, and if so what law does it follow?

Spring rate is constant and follows Hooke's law, which states that the deflection is directly proportional to the force producing it.

236. When referring to springs, what is meant by the following?
(a) **Natural frequency.** *(b)* **Amplitude.**

(a) This is the number of vibrations or oscillations per minute.

(b) This is the maximum movement from the mean position, i.e. half the maximum travel of the spring. It is usually measured in inches.

FRICTION AND CENTER OF GRAVITY

237. A simple trailer has its wheels mounted on a 4-in. dia shaft, running in plain bearings. If the coefficient of friction of each bearing is 0.06 and the load on each wheel is 2100 lb/ft., calculate in respect of each wheel: *(a)* **the frictional torque in lb/ft resisting rotation, and** *(b)* **the horsepower absorbed by friction at 300 R.P.M.**

$$\text{Retarding torque lb/ft} = \frac{\text{frictional force} \times \text{radius}}{12}$$

$$= \frac{\text{load} \times \mu \times 2}{12}$$

$$= \frac{2100 \times 0.06 \times 2}{12}$$

$$= 21 \text{ lb/ft}$$

$$\text{h.p.} = \frac{2\pi N T}{33000}$$

$$= \frac{2 \times 22 \times 300 \times 21}{7 \times 33000}$$

$$= 1.2 \text{ h.p.}$$

238. What is the center of gravity of a car, and how can its position, in the horizontal plane, be found?

The center of gravity of a car is a single point at which (for the purpose of convenience) the weight of the vehicle is said to be concentrated. Its position can be found by the principle of moments using the front and rear axle loadings and the wheel base.

239. A car weighing 1 ton has a 55/45 weight distribution. The wheelbase is 8 ft. Calculate how far the c.g. lies behind the front axle.

$$\text{Weight on front axle} = 55 \text{ per cent of 1 ton}$$

$$= \frac{55}{100} \times 20$$

$$= 11 \text{ cwt.}$$

$$\text{Weight on rear axle} = 45 \text{ per cent of 1 ton}$$

$$= \frac{45}{100} \times 20$$

$$= 9 \text{ cwt.}$$

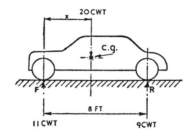

Taking moments about F,

Clockwise moment = anto-clockwise moment

$$x \times 20 = 8 \times 9$$

$$x = \frac{8 \times 9}{20}$$

$$= 3.6 \text{ ft}$$

$$= 3 \text{ ft. } 7.2 \text{ in.}$$

C.g. is 3 ft 7.2 in. behind front axle.

METALS

240. List ten metals commonly used in the construction of motor vehicles.

(a) Mild steel. *(b)* Cast iron. *(c)* Brass. *(d)* Copper. *(e)* High-tensile steel. *(f)* Aluminum alloy. *(g)* Lead. *(h)* Chromium. *(i)* Zinc-base die-casting alloys. *(j)* White metal.

241. Give an example of where each of the metals mentioned in the answer to the previous question may be used.

(*a*) Door panels. (*b*) Cylinder blocks. (*c*) Spring eye bushings. (*d*) Electric wiring cables. (*e*) Cylinder-head studs. (*f*) Cylinder heads. (*g*) Batteries. (*h*) On cylinder bores. (*i*) Carburetors. (*j*) Connecting rod bearings.

242. What are "ferrous" and "non-ferrous" metals?

A ferrous metal is one which contains iron as its main constituent. A non-ferrous metal is one which does not contain iron as its main constituent.

243. What is the difference between cast iron and steel?

Both these metals are (mainly) alloys of iron and carbon. Their main difference lies in their carbon content and its form in the metal. With 1.7 per cent carbon and above, the alloy is classed as cast iron, and some of the carbon is free. Below 1.7 per cent carbon, the alloy is classed as steel, and the carbon is in solution.

244. What are "plain carbon steels"?

These are steels which do not contain any special alloying constituents.

245. Name five alloying constituents for steel.

(*a*) Manganese. (*b*) Chromium. (*c*) Nickel. (*d*) Tungsten. (*e*) Vanadium.

246. What properties will the alloying constituents named in answer to the previous question confer on the steel with which they are alloyed?

(*a*) *Manganese:* Good work-hardening properties, acts as a deoxidizing agent, and combines with sulphur. Improves mechanical properties.

(*b*) *Chromium:* Improved resistance to heat and corrosion. Increased strength and hardness.

(*c*) *Nickel:* Improves hardening properties, strength, and ductility. Reduces temperature at which hardening can be carried out.

(*d*) *Tungsten:* Gives improved strength and hardness at high temperature.

(*e*) *Vanadium:* Improves fatigue life, strength, and elasticity.

247. What is full "annealing" and how is it carried out?

Annealing is a heating and cooling operation. The effect on a material is to soften it, for machining purposes, to relieve internal stresses, and to obtain refinement of the grain in combination with high ductility.

To anneal steel, heat to a cherry-red and cool slowly, e.g. in sand or in the furnace.

To anneal most non-ferrous metals, heat to a cherry-red and quench in water, or allow to cool slowly.

248. What is "normalizing," and how is it carried out?

Normalizing is the relieving of internal stresses such as may be set up by welding or cold working. It consists of heating the metal to a cherry-red and cooling in still air.

249. What is the object of case-hardening?

To provide a hard outer skin to resist wear and yet retain a tough inner core to resist shock loading.

250. Give an example of two engine components which may be case-hardened.

(a) Tappet blocks. (b) Wrist pins, piston pins.

251. What is the object of tempering steel, and how is it done?

Steel is tempered to improve its toughness. It is first heated to a cherry-red and then quenched. It is then heated to the required tempering temperature and again quenched.

252. Name three processes by which suitable steels may be hardened, and state one component on which each process might be used.

(a) Nitriding: Crankshafts. (b) Flame hardening: cam-shafts (c) High-frequency hardening: flywheel starter rings.

HARDNESS OF METALS AND HEAT TREATMENT

253. Place the following metals in descending order of hardness. Cast iron, mild steel, high carbon, copper, white metal.

High carbon steel, cast-iron, mild steel, copper, white metal.

254. How can the precise degree of hardness of a metal be determined?

It may be measured on a machine specially made for the purpose. According to type, an indentation is made in the metal by a hardened steel ball, diamond pyramid, or cone. The size of the indentation is measured and compared with a set of tables which give corresponding hardness values.

255. Suggest two common examples of heat treatment of metals that could be carried out in a motor vehicle repair workshop.

(a) Annealing (softening) copper pipe by heating to a cherry-red and then cooling.

(b) Case-hardening a mild steel pin, by making it red hot and immersing it in a carbon-rich powder.

256. What are two of the major problems associated with attempts to heat-treat various metals?

(a) That some of the properties of a metal may be destroyed.

(b) That uneven heating may set up differential expansion, that may lead to cracks occurring in the metal.

HEAT MEASUREMENT, FUEL H.P., AND THERMAL EFFICIENCY

257. How is heat normally measured?

(a) In British thermal units (Btu). One Btu is the amount of heat required to raise the temperature of 1 lb of water through 1 Fahrenheit degree.

(b) In Centigrade Heat Units (C.H.U.). One C.H.U. is the amount of heat required to raise the temperature of 1 lb of water through 1 Centigrade degree.

258. What is the mechanical equivalent of heat?

It is the amount of work equivalent to 1 unit of heat.

1 Btu   = 778 ft/lb
1 C.H.U. = 1400 ft/lb

259. What is the approximate brake thermal efficiency of a gasoline engine?

23 per cent.

260. What is the approximate brake thermal efficiency of a Diesel engine?

34 per cent.

261. What is the formula used to calculate the fuel horse-power of an engine?

$$\text{Fuel h.p.} = \frac{\text{Weight of fuel used per minute} \times \text{calorific value of fuel} \times \text{Joule's equivalent}}{33,000}$$

262. What is meant by the calorific value of a fuel?
This is the total heat that will be liberated when the fuel is completely burned. It is expressed in Btu's or C.H.U.'s per pound.

263. What is the formula used to determine the heat given out by or required by a substance when its temperature falls or is raised?
Heat required (or given out) = weight of substance × its specific heat × temperature change

CENTRIFUGAL FORCE

264. Explain simply what is meant by centrifugal force?
A force which acts radially outwards from a center.

265. Give three examples where centrifugal force is usefully employed on a motor vehicle.
(a) The advance and retard mechanism of many distributors. (b) Some automatic clutches. (c) The governor mechanism on certain C.I. engine fuel-injection pumps.

266. What formula is used to calculate centrifugal force?

Centrifugal force $= \dfrac{Wv^2}{gr}$

where W = weight in pounds

v = velocity in feet per second

g = 32.2

r = radius of rotation in feet.

TRIGONOMETRY

267. For the triangle as shown, in terms of the lettered sides, what will be (a) the sine, (b) the cosine, (c) the tangent of angle A?

(a) Sine of angle A $= \dfrac{a}{c}$

(b) Cosine of angle A $= \dfrac{b}{c}$

(c) Tangent of angle A $= \dfrac{a}{b}$

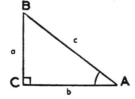

MECHANICAL ADVANTAGE AND VELOCITY
RATIO OF HYDRAULIC SYSTEM

268. If the area of a piston of a hydraulic master-cylinder is
2 in² and it is being forced inward with a force of 300 lb, find:
(a) The pressure, in lb psi, set up in the system. (b) The force
acting on the wheel cylinder piston if its area is 3 in².

(a) Pressure $= \dfrac{\text{load}}{\text{area}} = \dfrac{300}{2} = 150$ lb psi.

(b) Force = area × pressure = 3 × 150 = 450 lb.

269. What is the mechanical advantage of the hydraulic system
mentioned in the previous question?

Mechanical advantage $= \dfrac{\text{load}}{\text{effort}}$

$= \dfrac{450}{150}$

$= 3:1$

270. If a master-cylinder piston travels two inches to apply the
brakes, whilst the total travel of the wheel-cylinder pistons is
0.25 in., what is the velocity ratio of the system?

Velocity ratio $= \dfrac{\text{movement at input}}{\text{movement at output}}$

$= \dfrac{2}{0.25} = 8:1$

ELECTRICAL
IGNITION

*See also Questions 186 to 194 First Year and Questions 122 to
130 Second Year.*

271. **Why is a ballast resistor used in series with the ignition
coil?**

When the engine is started, the resistance is automatically by-
passed. This permits a higher current to flow in the coil primary
circuit. It produces a hotter spark to give fast starting.

NOTE: A special type coil is used in conjunction with a ballast
resistor.

272. What is the difference between the primary and secondary windings of an ignition coil?

The primary winding consists of only a few hundred turns of comparatively thick wire. The secondary winding consists of many thousands of turns of very fine wire.

273. What are three main advantages of transistorized ignition systems?

(a) Suitable for very high-speed engines.

(b) Very light current passes through contact points which gives long life, with no pitting or burning. Also no condenser is necessary.

(c) Timing of spark can be more precise than with ordinary distributor/coil ignition system.

274. Does a high-tension spark occur when the contact-breaker points open or when they close?

When the contact-breaker points open.

275. Why is an oscilloscope considered so superior to the "old-fashioned" methods of ignition testing?

The behavior of the entire ignition system can be observed pictorially under actual operating conditions, while the engine is running.

276. What is "dwell" as referred to in connection with ignition systems?

It is the number of degrees of distributor cam rotation during which the points are closed.

STARTER MOTORS

277. Why are many starter motors now controlled by a solenoid switch in preference to a heavy-duty, direct-acting switch?

(a) The action of the electrically-operated solenoid switch is much faster than a manually-operated switch. Thus the period of time when arcing between the contacts can occur is much less, and consequently switch life is prolonged.

(b) Ignition key-operated switches would be impossible without solenoid operation.

(c) Where remotely controlled switches can reduce starter-lead length, voltage drop in the cables will be smaller.

(d) A remotely controlled solenoid switch can be fitted to avoid the long heavy-gauge cables that would otherwise be necessary.

278. Approximately what may be the maximum current flow to a starter-motor during its operation?

In the region of 200-400 amp for a commercial vehicle, 100-200 amp for a car.

279. The p.d. of a battery supplying 300 amp to a starter-motor is 10V. If the resistance of the battery leads is 0.0045 ohm, what will be *(a)* **the voltage drop in the starter lead, and** *(b)* **the voltage across the starter terminals?**

(a) Voltage drop $= I \times R$
$$\text{or } E = I \times R$$
$$= 300 \times 0.0045$$
$$= 1.35\text{V}$$

(b) Voltage at starter $= 10 - 1.35 = 8.65\text{V}$

280. Is the current flow from the battery to the starter-motor constant all the time the starter is rotating?

No. Initially a high current is required, but this rapidly drops as the starter-motor speeds up.

281. What is an "inertia drive" starter?

This really refers to the method of pinion engagement with the flywheel. As the motor commences to revolve initially, the pinion, due to its inertia (in this case reluctance to revolve) slides on a very coarse thread, along the armature shaft, until it is in mesh with flywheel ring gear. (See illustration below.)

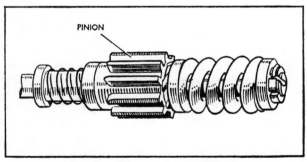

An inertia-engaged starter drive

282. Many starter-motor pinions are fitted with a strong spring. What is the purpose of this spring?

To reduce shock loading at the moment engagement takes place.

283. If the starter-motor whirrs round when operated yet does not engage and turn the engine, what might be the trouble?

(a) If it whirrs vigorously and the battery is charged up, the starter pinion is probably sticking on its sleeve. The starter will have to be removed and the pinion drive cleaned.

(b) A sluggish whirring probably indicates an almost dead battery, together with a slightly sticking pinion.

284. How can the voltage drop in a starter lead and switch be determined?

(a) Place a voltmeter across the battery terminals.

(b) Place another voltmeter between the end of the battery lead (where it bolts on to the starter) and ground.

(c) Operate the starter-motor and simultaneously note the readings on the two voltmeters.

(d) The difference in the readings is the voltage drop in the lead.

FOURTH YEAR

MOTOR VEHICLE TECHNOLOGY

COMPRESSION-IGNITION ENGINE

1. Describe briefly the compression-ignition (or diesel) cycle (four stroke).

Intake: The piston descends, drawing only air into the cylinder.

Compression: The piston rises, compressing the air to a temperature well above the ignition temperature of the fuel, and the fuel ignites as it is sprayed in just before t.d.c.

Power: The high temperature of the burning fuel causes high gas pressures, which force the piston downward.

Exhaust: The rising piston expels the exhaust gases.

2. How is the speed and power output of a compression-ignition engine controlled?

By varying the quantity of fuel delivered by the injectors. The amount of air taken in per stroke remains (roughly) the same under all conditions, and these engines are said to be "quality governed."

3. What is the approximate compression ratio of compression-ignition engines?

The figure varies according to the design of a particular engine, but will almost certainly be between 12:1 and 20:1.

4. What are the approximate values of pressure and temperature attained by the compressed air at the end of the compression stroke in a C.I. engine?

This depends upon the condition of the engine and its compression ratio. Typical values are: air pressure 600 lbs psi, and air temperature 675°C.

5. Give five advantages of a compression-ignition engine as compared with a gasoline engine.

(a) Higher thermal efficiency. *(b)* Less fire risk with diesel fuel than with gasoline. *(c)* Good torque at low speeds. *(d)* Less minor

maintenance required on injection equipment than on spark-ignition equipment. *(e)* A C.I. engine will usually run for longer periods between overhauls.

6. Give five disadvantages of a compression-ignition engine as against a gasoline engine.

(a) Higher initial cost. *(b)* Rougher running, particularly at idling speeds. *(c)* For a given power output a C.I. engine will be heavier and bulkier than a comparable gasoline engine. *(d)* Noisier, particularly at low r.p.m. *(e)* Maximum r.p.m. is less.

7. How do the following components in a gasoline engine compare with their counterparts in a similar sized C.I. engine: pistons, bearing materials, connecting rods, and cylinder blocks?

(a) Pistons: Heavier, stouter and are almost always made of aluminum alloy. *(b) Bearing materials:* Harder (and more expensive) to withstand heavier loads. *(c) Connecting rods:* Normally stronger and heavier. *(d) Cylinder block:* Normally stronger and heavier.

8. What is the object of 'squish' and 'swirl'?

Squish and swirl are carefully directed air movements within the cylinder. The object of this air movement is to provide good turbulence, particularly during combustion. Air movement across the fuel spray removes the products of combustion from the burning particles of fuel and replaces them with unburnt air. This turbulence is very important in the interests of smooth running and economy.

9. What is the object of a masked inlet valve?

To direct the flow of air entering the cylinder during induction and so promote swirl.

10. How may squish action be obtained?

By shaping the piston crown as shown. The squish action is shown by the arrows above the piston.

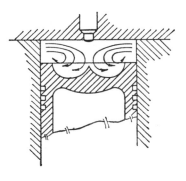

11. Explain the difference between a direct-injection and an indirect-injection engine.

A direct-injection engine is one in which the fuel is injected directly into the combustion space above and/or in the piston.

An indirect-injection engine is one in which the fuel is injected into an ante-chamber, connected to the main combustion space by a restricted throat or passage.

12. State four advantages of direct-injection engines as compared with indirect-injection engines.

(a) More economical. (b) Easier starting due to lower heat losses. (c) More complete scavenging. (d) Higher mechanical efficiency.

13. State four advantages of indirect-injection engines as compared with direct-injection engines.

(a) Less sensitive to fuel quality. (b) Smoother running due to lower rate of pressure rise. (c) Softer spray and lower pressure produce less wear and tear on the injection equipment. (d) Lighter pistons assist in obtaining higher r.p.m.

14. With two-stroke gasoline engines a certain amount of new mixture leaves the cylinder with the outgoing exhaust gases and this is one of the major reasons for its inefficiency. How is this problem avoided with a two-stroke C.I. engine?

Only air enters the cylinder during intake of the two-stroke C.I. cycle. Fuel is not injected until all the ports and/or valves are closed.

15. Why is it that supercharging is particularly popular with manufacturers of two-stroke C.I. engines?

The blast of pressurized air entering the cylinder helps to insure rapid and thorough scavenging of the exhaust gases, and good filling of the cylinder with a charge of clean air.

16. State three of the main advantages of a two-stroke C.I. engine over a four-stroke C.I. engine.

(a) Higher power output for a given space and weight. (b) Smoother torque output. (c) Lighter flywheel which facilitates gear changing.

17. What are the three phases of combustion in the C.I. engine?

(1) The delay period, when the injected fuel just starts to burn, but without producing any significant rise in pressure.

(2) The second phase, when the whole of the fuel then present in the cylinder burns very rapidly, resulting in a steep rise in cylinder pressure.

(3) The final phase when the fuel burns as it leaves the injector.

18. Which of the three phases of combustion causes 'diesel knock'?

The second phase when a very steep and rapid pressure rise occurs in the cylinder.

19. What is the most important single quality of a diesel fuel?

Its ignition quality, i.e. its readiness for self-ignition with the least possible delay after leaving the injector.

20. How may the ignition quality of a C.I. engine fuel be expressed for purposes of comparison?

By reference to its 'Cetane Number,' or its 'Diesel Index.'

21. What would be a typical ignition temperature for fuel oil?

400°C.

22. What is the difference between a P.V. diagram and a pressure crank-angle diagram?

Both are, in effect, graphs, however:

(a) A P.V. diagram indicates cylinder pressure (shown vertically) against piston position, i.e. cylinder volume (shown horizontally).

(b) A pressure crank-angle diagram, indicates cylinder pressure (shown vertically) against degrees of crankshaft rotation (shown horizontally).

23. Why is it especially important that valve timing on a C.I. engine is correct, even before starting the engine?

In most C.I. engines, the clearance between the valve head and the piston crown is very small. If the engine was rotated with incorrect valve timing, serious damage to the valves and pistons could result.

24. What is one practical method of checking the clearance existing between the valves and the piston crown on a C.I. engine?

With the head removed, place a piece of soft lead wire on the piston crown, immediately below each valve. Replace the head and rotate the engine gently by hand. The wire will be squeezed to the thickness of the space between the valve and piston. Remove the head and measure the thickness of the wire.

25. Assuming that the vehicle is being fed with the correct grade and type of fuel oil, what is the most important single item of maintenance in the vehicle's fuel supply system?

Insuring that the fuel is being correctly filtered before it reaches the injector pump.

26. What main types of filter element material are used to filter fuel oil?

(a) Resin impregnated paper (now very widely used because of its effectiveness in removing minute particles). (b) Felt.

27. What types of fuel lift pumps are used on C.I. engines?

(a) Mechanically operated diaphragm pumps very similar to their gasoline pump counterparts. (b) Mechanically operated plunger-type pumps.

IN-LINE TYPE INJECTOR PUMP

28. How many pumping elements will an in-line injector pump for a six-cylinder engine contain?

Six, one for each cylinder.

29. What two parts make up a pumping element?

The plunger and the barrel.

30. What is the function of a delivery valve in an injector pump?

(a) To act as a non-return valve and thus prevent fuel from being drawn out of the pipe line and injector when the pump plunger is on the down stroke.

(b) To act as an anti-dribble device.

31. What is 'phasing' of injector pumps?

Testing, and if necessary adjusting, an injector pump to insure that each pumping element causes injection at exactly the correct interval of degrees after the preceding element. For instance, with a four-element pump, injections must take place at exactly $90°$ intervals, and with a six-element pump at $60°$ intervals.

32. What is 'calibration' of injector pumps?

Testing and, if required, adjusting an injector pump to insure that it is delivering the correct amount of fuel at various speeds and rack settings, and that each element is supplying an equal amount of fuel.

33. During a phasing check one element is causing late injection. How can this be remedied?

By raising the tappet of that particular element.

34. How can the quantity of fuel delivered by one pumping element be varied without altering the amount delivered by the other elements in the same pump?

By loosening the toothed collar on the plunger sleeve and rotating the sleeve slightly, relative to the collar.

35. Briefly describe the operation of 'spill' phasing.

The pump main gallery must be gravity fed from approximately a 2-ft head and a degree ring fitted to the pump camshaft.

Secure the rack at about its mid-position. Remove the delivery valve and spring of No. 1 element and fit an open-ended swan-necked pipe to that element. Turn on the fuel supply and rotate the pump camshaft in the correct direction of rotation.

With the plunger[1] rising slowly from b.d.c., note the point on the degree ring at which fuel just ceases to flow from the swan-necked pipe. (This must coincide with the manufacturer's timing mark for No. 1 injection.)

Replace the delivery valve and repeat the foregoing procedure for the remaining pumping elements in the order of firing.

Adjust the tappets, if necessary, to insure correct injection intervals, as mentioned in the answer to Question 31.

[1]Note: Plunger head clearance must always be within manufacturers' recommended limits.

36. To what degree of accuracy must the following operations be carried out? *(a)* Phasing. *(b)* The balancing of the outputs of the pumping elements during calibration.

(a) To within $\pm \frac{1}{2}°$. *(b)* To within ± 2 per cent.

37. Name two common types of injector pump governors.

(a) Centrifugal. *(b)* Pneumatic or vacuum.

38. Explain briefly the main differences between the mechanical (centrifugal) and pneumatic (vacuum) governors.

In the centrifugal governor the action of the centrifugal weights controls rack position only at idling and maximum r.p.m. At intermediate speeds the rack is under the direct control of the accelerator.

The vacuum governor is controlled by intake vacuum, and it controls the rack position at all loads and speeds. The rack is in no way directly connected to the accelerator.

39. When an engine which is controlled by a vacuum governor is stopped, what position will the fuel rack be in?
In the maximum delivery position.

DISTRIBUTOR TYPE FUEL PUMP

40. Briefly describe a distributor type pump.
Externally it resembles somewhat, in size and shape, the distributor of a gasoline engine. It has a single pumping element which serves all the cylinders. Distribution to the various injectors being via a rotary distributor which connects with the outlet branches in the correct firing order.

41. What type of governor may be fitted to a distributor type injection pump?
An all-speed hydraulic or mechanical governor.

42. Give six advantages of the distributor type fuel pump, over the in-line pump.
(*a*) Reciprocating masses are small so that higher r.p.m. is easily obtainable.
(*b*) Cheaper.
(*c*) More compact.
(*d*) Cannot inject if engine tries to run in reverse rotation.
(*e*) Very little power needed to drive it and torsional vibration is much reduced.
(*f*) Can be fitted into a distributor drive socket so that similar cylinder blocks can be used for both spark ignition and C.I. engines.

INJECTORS AND COLD STARTING

43. Name three types of injector nozzle.
(*a*) Single-hole. (*b*) Multi-hole. (*c*) Pintaux.

44. Explain briefly the function of a pintaux nozzle.
The pintaux nozzle was designed mainly to assist in cold starting without the need for heater plugs. It provides different spray characteristics for cranking speeds and engine running speeds, the characteristics being matched to the differing requirements.

45. What is the purpose of an injector leak-off?
In service a certain amount of fuel must leak past the needle valve stem and into the body of the injector. If a leak-off was not

provided the needle would, in time, be unable to lift properly, because the space above the needle would be filled with fuel.

46. List five symptoms which might indicate that an injector pump required servicing.

(a) Black exhaust smoke. (b) Rough idling. (c) Loss of power. (d) High fuel consumption. (e) Heavy carbon deposits in combustion chamber.

47. List four symptoms of a faulty injector.

(a) Engine missing on one cylinder. (b) Black exhaust smoke. (c) Loss of power. (d) Knocking.

48. At what injection pressures do the following engines usually operate? (a) Direct-injection engines. (b) Indirect-injection engines.

(a) About 175 atmospheres. (b) About 120 atmospheres.

49. What do the above figures represent in pounds per square inch?

(a) 120 atmospheres = 120 × 14.7 = 1764 lbs psi.
(b) 175 atmospheres = 175 × 14.7 = 2572.5 lbs psi.

50. What is an 'excess delivery' device, and what does it do?

This is the name of a device (there are many types) fitted to a fuel pump to give an extra supply of fuel to the injectors during starting. The injection period is prolonged and this increases the chances of ignition.

51. Name three aids to cold starting excluding excess delivery devices used on a C.I. engine.

(a) Heater plugs. (b) Ki-gas intake manifold heater. (c) Ether spray.

52. What is a decompression device and what is its function?

It is a means of preventing compression occurring inside the cylinder (usually by holding open the inlet valve). This then allows the engine to be rotated easily and when the flywheel has gathered sufficient momentum, the device can be 'switched off': compression then occurs in the normal way and the engine should start, helped greatly by the flywheel momentum overcoming compression pressure.

SUPERCHARGERS AND COMPRESSION RATIO

53. What is a supercharger and where is it fitted?

Put simply, it is a pump or compressor which, on a spark ignition engine, is usually placed between the carburetor and inlet manifold. On a C.I. engine it feeds air directly into the intake manifold or passages.

54. What is the object of supercharging an engine?

To obtain a greater power output from a given size of engine by improving the volumetric efficiency of the engine (i.e. by better filling of the cylinders than is possible under normal atmospheric conditions).

55. What other advantages are there in supercharging a gasoline engine?

(a) Engine torque is improved over whole speed range.

(b) Faster acceleration.

(c) Where the supercharger is fitted with an automatic lubrication system, this lubricant eventually passes into the cylinder and can be useful as upper cylinder lubricant.

(d) Improved mixing of the fuel and air.

56. What specific advantages are there in supercharging a C.I. engine?

(a) Reduction in diesel knock. (b) Better torque especially at low r.p.m. (c) Running is smoother and quieter. (d) Elimination of exhaust smoke especially during low speed acceleration. (e) Improved cold starting.

57. What, in general, are the disadvantages of superchargers?

(a) Expense. (b) Additional complication. (c) Vacuum-operated accessories (on a gasoline engine), e.g. vacuum wipers, cannot be used. (d) Cooling system must be able to accommodate greater heat output.

58. Approximately what is the boost pressure created by a supercharger?

It varies from about 4 PPSI to 30 PPSI according to type and application.

59. Name these three widely used types of superchargers.

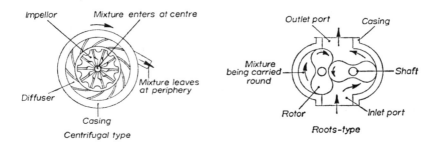

Impellor   Mixture enters at centre

Mixture leaves at periphery

Diffuser

Casing

Centrifugal type

Outlet port   Casing

Mixture being carried round

Shaft

Rotor   Inlet port

Roots-type

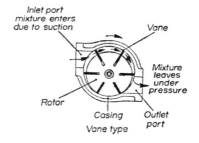

Inlet port mixture enters due to suction   Vane

Mixture leaves under pressure

Rotor

Casing   Outlet port

Vane type

(*a*) Centrifugal. (*b*) Roots (*not* Rootes). (*c*) Vane.

60. What effect will raising the compression ratio have on the power output of an engine?

Engine power will increase (provided there are no side-effects, e.g. detonation, in a gasoline engine).

INDEPENDENT SUSPENSION

See Third Year Questions 181 to 184.

61. Why is independent suspension applied only to the front wheels in the vast majority of motor cars?

The reason is primarily one of cost. Further, the benefits obtained from independent rear suspension, as compared with the conventional type of rear axle, are not so great as they are when i.f.s. is substituted for a beam-type front axle.

62. What are the advantages of independent rear suspension?

(*a*) Reduced unsprung weight, giving a better ride. (*b*) Improved weight distribution is possible, in some cases, by combining transmission and rear axle. (c) Freedom from 'axle tramp' and similar troubles. (d) No wheel lift due to transmission torque. (e) Increased useful space within the car.

63. What are the disadvantages of independent rear suspension?
(a) Increased cost. (b) More moving parts. (c) With some types, under certain conditions, steering can be adversely affected.

64. How is steering geometry and tire wear affected by spring deflection with unequal length wishbone-type suspension?
(a) Camber varies slightly, but (usually) castor action is little affected.
(b) Tire tends to be scrubbed sideways only slightly.

65. How is steering geometry and tire wear affected by spring deflection with swing axle type independent suspension?
(a) Camber varies considerably.
(b) Track varies slightly as tires are scrubbed sideways. (Rate of tire wear can be high.)

66. With parallel trailing link independent suspension, what effect does spring deflection have on steering geometry and tire wear?
The wheelbase on one (or both) sides may vary slightly. None of the steering angles should be affected. The effect on tire wear should be negligible.

67. With the conventional beam axle and Hotchkiss drive layout the driving and braking forces are transmitted to the frame through the semi-elliptic springs. How can these forces be transmitted on a car with independent rear suspension and fitted with coil springs?
Through the suspension arms and their pivots fixed to the frame. In some cases it is necessary to fit special torque arms to locate the axle and take driving and braking forces.

STEERING

68. Name four types of steering gear in general use.
(a) Recirculating ball. (b) Worm and sector. (c) Rack-and-pinion. (d) Cam-and-peg.

69. How can the recirculating ball-type steering gear be adjusted?

Axial adjustment of the worm is by shims between the end plate and the housing. An adjustment bolt (or shims under the top cover plate) may adjust the position of the rocker-shaft relative to the steering nut.

70. How may the worm-and-sector steering gear be adjusted?

Axial movement of the worm can be taken up by removing shims from between the end plate and the steering-box main housing. Backlash is commonly adjustable by mounting the sector shaft in a separate casing which can be moved relative to the worm. This has the effect of moving the teeth on the sector farther into, or farther out of, mesh with the worm.

71. How can the rack-and-pinion steering gear be adjusted?

Axial adjustment of the pinion is generally by shims. Backlash between the teeth of the rack and the pinion may be controlled, in some cases, by moving the rack towards the pinion. In some well-known designs backlash between the teeth is controlled automatically by spring-loading the rack towards the pinion.

72. How can the cam-and-peg steering gear be adjusted?

Axial movement of the shaft can be taken up by removing shims fitted between the end plate and main housing. Free play can be taken up by means of the adjusting screw on the cover plate. This screw can be used to force the conical peg more deeply into the tapered groove of the cam track.

73. What is the approximate gear ratio (or angular ratio) used in a motor-car steering housing?

This varies in accordance with the size and weight of the car and the design of the steering mechanism, but is generally between about 12:1 and 10:1.

74. On a vehicle with its steering mechanism in good condition, approximately how much play should there be, measured at the rim of the steering wheel?

Approximately 1 in.

75. If there is too much free play at the steering wheel, how can it be determined whether or not the play is in the steering-housing?

First insure the Pitman arm is securely fitted on to the cross-shaft, or rocker shaft. Then, while holding the Pitman-arms stationary, check the free movement now remaining at the rim of the steering wheel.

76. **How can a steering ball joint be checked for excessive free play?**

When the rod adjacent to the joint is gripped, it should be possible to twist the rod slightly, but there should be no clearance or play in the joint.

77. **How are front wheel bearings adjusted?**

Wheels with taper roller bearings may be adjusted as follows:

(*i*) With the wheel jacked up, and the wheel bearings and nut in position on the spindle, gradually tighten up the nut until the wheel spins quite freely but there is no play. The brakes must not bind at all during this operation.

(*ii*) Turn the nut backwards until the nearest slot on the nut lines up with the cotter pin hole, pin the nut to the spindle with a snug-fitting pin and open out the legs of the pin. (The maximum backward turn of the nut is no more than one-sixth of a turn, i.e. from one cotter pin hole to the next.)

(*iii*) This should leave a slight amount of play in the bearing (no more than about 1/16 in. at the outer circumference of the tire) which is desirable. Check to see that the adjustment has been correctly made.

Note: Wheels with either ball-bearings or parallel roller bearings are not adjustable, and the wheel nut should be tightened securely and (usually) cotter pinned into position.

78. **What are the main causes of undue shock or tremor felt through the steering wheel?**

(*a*) Car travelling on a rough surface. (*b*) Wheels require balancing. (*c*) On rack-and-pinion type steering, e.g. Morris Minor, the steering damper may require adjustment. (*d*) Excessive free play. (*e*) Faulty front shock-absorbers. (*f*) Where the car has a three-piece track rod layout, wheel tremor can result if the two outer rods have been adjusted wrongly so that they are of unequal length. (*g*) Loose or broken spring shackles or suspension mountings.

79. **What may cause a vehicle to wander?**

(*a*) Low or uneven tire pressure. (*b*) Too much weight at the rear end. (*c*) Excessive free play in the steering. (*d*) Weak shock-absorbers or springs. (*e*) Stiff king-pin bearings. (*f*) Steering or suspension misalignment (perhaps caused by a severe blow).

80. **What are the main causes of stiff steering?**

(*a*) Insufficient lubrication of the king-pins or steering linkage. (*b*) Tire pressures too low. (*c*) Wheels out of track, i.e. toe-in not correct. (d) Stiffness in the steering column itself, caused by lack of lubricant or overtight adjustment.

81. What are 'oversteer' and 'understeer'?

Oversteer is the tendency of a vehicle to turn into a bend and has to be counteracted by 'paying off' the steering lock.

Understeer is the tendency of a vehicle to run wide on bends and has to be counteracted by applying more lock.

82. How do the slip angles of the front and rear tires affect oversteer and understeer?

With the slip angle at the front greater than that at the rear, the car will understeer.

With the slip angle at the rear greater than that at the front, the car will oversteer.

83. What is the slip angle of a tire?

It is the angle between the direction in which the tire is aimed and the actual direction in which it travels.

84. Suggest two practical methods of reducing oversteer.

(a) Reduce rear end weight. (b) Increase rear and/or reduce front tire pressures.

85. Give five reasons why power steering on cars has become much more popular in recent years.

(a) More weight is now carried by front wheels. (b) Wider section tires give more drag, especially when manœuvring at low speeds. (c) Parking is more difficult in that considerably more low speed manœuvring is frequently called for. (d) Reduction of driver's effort leaves him more alert. (e) With some larger cars, steering gear ratio would require to be abnormally low if power assistance was not provided.

86. What are the basic operating principles of an hydraulically operated, power-assisted steering system?

A double acting 'slave' cylinder is connected to the steering linkage. Movement of the steering wheel actuates a valve which allows high pressure oil to force the slave cylinder piston (and steering linkage) in the required direction. The hydraulic mechanism is so arranged that movement of the slave cylinder piston (and steering linkage) is always proportional to steering wheel movement.

87. If the hydraulic assistance on a power steering mechanism failed, would it still be possible to operate the steering?
Yes, but the effort needed at the steering wheel would be very considerable.

BRAKES

See Third Year Questions 195-211.

88. Name three types of adjusters found on drum brakes.
(a) Eccentric. *(b)* Micram adjuster. *(c)* Wedge and plungers.

89. What is the object of fitting automatic brake adjusters (i.e. self-adjusting brakes)?
To maintain an approximately constant minimum clearance between the braking surfaces. This has the benefit of keeping brake pedal travel to a minimum and reducing maintenance.

90. What type of brake is virtually always self-adjusting?
The disc brake.

91. What is the function of a pressure limiting valve and where is it fitted?
Its function is to limit the pressure applied to the rear brakes in order to prevent locking of the rear wheels under hard braking. It is fitted in the hydraulic brake line leading to the rear brakes.

92. What is the difference between a power-operated and a power-assisted braking system?
With a power-operated system the brake pedal merely operates a valve which allows air, vacuum, or hydraulic pressure to actuate the brakes. There is no direct connection between the pedal and the brakes themselves.
With a power-assisted system, the effort of the driver in applying the brakes is *assisted* by some kind of power mechanism.

93. Name three ways of producing the power effort required by a power-assisted braking system.
(a) Vacuum, from the intake manifold or a separate exhauster (vacuum pump). *(b)* Hydraulic pressure supplied by an engine-driven pump. *(c)* Air pressure, again supplied by an engine-driven pump.

94. Give three reasons why power brakes are becoming so popular on cars.

(a) Reduces driver's effort, particularly important with lady drivers.

(b) Disc brakes often have no 'self-servo' effect (as have drum brakes) and consequently higher pedal pressures are needed for equal retardation.

(c) Harder, longer lasting, and more fade-free friction material can be used if sufficient effort is available to overcome their lower coefficient of friction.

95. What effect does temperature rise have on the coefficient of friction of brake-linings?

Provided the temperature remains within the stable range of the material, little effect will be noticed. When temperature goes beyond the point at which the material becomes unstable, the coefficient of friction falls rapidly.

96. What will be the braking torque supplied by a disc brake which has friction pads on each side of the disc at a mean radius of 3 in., when the force on the pads is 1,000 lb and the pad/disc coefficient of friction is 0.25?

Braking torque = Force × coefficient of friction × radius
× number of friction faces

$$= 1,000 \times 0.25 \times \frac{3}{12} \times 2$$

$$= 125 \text{ ft lbs.}$$

FLUID FLYWHEEL

97. When a fluid flywheel is fitted to a vehicle, what component does it replace?

A fluid flywheel takes the place of the conventional clutch.

98. What type of fluid is used in a fluid flywheel?

Good-quality light engine oil.

99. What are the advantages of a fluid flywheel?

(a) Drive is taken up extremely smoothly.

(b) Torsional vibrations of crankshaft and transmission are dampened out. This, plus (a), greatly reduces wear and tear on transmission.

(c) The rotating parts are not subject to shock loads. Consequently little maintenance is required. Wear can only take place at the bearings and at the oil seal.

100. What are the disadvantages of a fluid flywheel?

(a) Not suitable for use with conventional-type transmission, because of persistent drag, even at very low r.p.m.

(b) Even under most favorable conditions, slight slip (about 2 per cent) occurs.

101. What are the two most probable causes for abnormal slip with a fluid flywheel?

(a) Lack of oil. (b) Use of incorrect viscosity oil.

102. What maintenance is required by a fluid flywheel?

Keep it filled with the correct grade of light oil up to the height of the level plug.

TORQUE CONVERTERS, AUTOMATIC TRANSMISSION AND PLANETARY GEARS

103. What is a 'torque converter'?

It is similar to a fluid flywheel with, in its simplest form, the addition of a non-rotating 'reaction member.' It provides, within limits, an infinitely variable gear ratio.

104. Where is a torque converter used?

As an integral part of a fully automatic transmission.

105. What is a 'fully automatic' transmission?

This is where the car has no clutch pedal and, in the normal sense, no gear lever. Gear changing up and down is fully automatic, as is the take-up of the drive.

106. Briefly describe a simple form of automatic transmission.

It could consist of a single stage (i.e. one reaction member) torque converter, coupled to one or more planetary gear trains. The torque converter acting as described in Question 103 while the gears are engaged automatically, in accordance with road speed and driver requirements (as signalled via the position of the accelerator pedal).

107. Give three reasons why planetary gears are so very widely used in automatic transmissions.

(*a*) They are always in constant mesh.

(*b*) Engagement may be obtained smoothly and quietly by the application of brake bands and clutches.

(*c*) A considerable variety of ratios and forward and reverse gears can be obtained (by design) from only one (or more) planetary gear train(s).

108. Name the main parts of a simple planetary gear train and show one example of how it works.

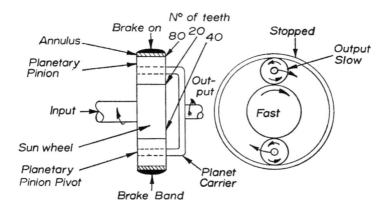

(*a*) Annulus or ring gear. (*b*) Planet pinions. (*c*) Planet carrier. (*d*) Sun gear.

OVERDRIVE

109. What is an overdrive?

A device which gives a higher ratio than that provided by the final drive.

110. Whereabouts in the transmission is an overdrive fitted?

In a housing bolted on to the rear of the transmission.

111. How is the overdrive gear engaged or disengaged by the driver?

American units use a detent plunger which is controlled by a solenoid which in turn is controlled by a manual electrical switch and/or a vacuum operated switch, controlled by the carburetor. In some cases where the overdrive unit consists of a dual-ratio rear-end, it may be actuated either hydraulically or by vacuum from the engine intake system.

112. What type of gearing is used in an overdrive?
A planetary gear train.

113. What are the advantages of an overdrive?
(a) A higher top gear, giving greater fuel economy.
(b) For a given road speed, engine r.p.m. is less; thus engine wear and tear is reduced.
(c) Reduced engine r.p.m. gives quieter running.
(d) Engagement and disengagement of overdrive is particularly easy.
(e) Overdrive is often operable in the indirect gears, giving an additional choice of ratios.

FINAL DRIVE SYSTEMS –
HEAVY COMMERCIAL VEHICLES

114. What is the purpose of a 'third differential,' and where is it fitted?
A third differential is placed in the transmission line between two live axles as fitted on some heavy commercial vehicles. Its purpose is to prevent 'wind up' in the transmission due to turning corners or to the use of tires of differing diameters. Thus tire wear and transmission wear and tear will be minimized.

115. Name two ways of obtaining the low final drive ratios normally required on heavy commercial vehicles.
(a) Worm and wheel. (b) Double reduction gearing.

116. What are the advantages of the worm-and-wheel type of final drive?
(a) Silent in operation. (b) Very long life. (c) Low gear ratios of down to 15:1 can be obtained. (d) Worm may be mounted above or below the worm wheel to give either low body line or good propeller-shaft ground clearance as desired. (e) No special lubrication problems.

117. What are the disadvantages of the worm-gear type of final drive?
(a) High cost. (The worm wheel is made of phosphor bronze.)
(b) This type of gearing is heavier than either the spiral bevel or the hypoid. (c) With some designs their mechanical efficiency is low.

118. What formula is used to calculate the gear ratio of a worm and wheel?

$$\text{Gear ratio} = \frac{\text{number of teeth on worm wheel}}{\text{number of starts on worm}}$$

119. Suggest two methods of obtaining double reduction final drive.

(a) One gear reduction at the center of the axle (e.g. master gear and pinion) driving a step-down planetary gear located in each wheel hub.

(b) A normal master gear and pinion, with the pinion shaft driven by a pair of step-down gears.

120. If a vehicle is said to have 'multi-drive' axles, what does this mean?

That more than one axle is driven. For example, it is usual to convey drive to both rear axles of an 'eight-wheeler' heavy commercial vehicle.

121. What are two types of multi-drive axle arrangements?

(a) Worm and wheel drive to each axle. An intermediate shaft secured to the rear of the forward worm, drives the rear worm.

(b) Master gear and pinion drive to each axle. Drive to the rearmost axle being provided via an additional pinion driven from the trailing edge of the foremost master gear.

122. Broadly speaking what are the two most important factors to consider when reassembling a final drive unit.

(a) That the teeth are correctly meshed.

(b) That the bearings are correctly pre-loaded (if pre-loading is required).

123. What is 'pre-loading' of bearings?

Setting up bearings so that they will rotate freely without any free play and then further tightening the adjustment to the manufacturer's specifications.

124. Which type of bearings can be pre-loaded?

Taper roller bearings only.

125. What are the advantages of pre-loading taper roller bearings?

(a) Increased resistance to shock loads. (b) Longer bearing life, because of (a). (c) Accurate maintenance of shaft position.

126. The full floating axle is used by a majority of commercial vehicles. What are its important features?

(*a*) With this axle design the axle shaft takes no loads except driving and engine-braking torques.

(*b*) The axle-shafts may be withdrawn without removing wheels or hub.

(*c*) The vehicle may be safely towed with a broken half-shaft (provided the broken piece or pieces of shaft will themselves not cause any further damage) or even no axle-shaft at all.

(*d*) It is more expensive, bulkier, and heavier than either of the other two types.

DAMPERS

127. What is the function of a suspension, or spring, damper?

To dampen out the oscillations (vibrations) of the road spring and to check rebound.

128. Dampers are often called shock-absorbers, but do they actually absorb any shock when, for example, the road wheel strikes an obstacle or drops into a pothole?

No. Although sometimes called 'shock-absorbers,' they do not principally absorb road shocks. This is done by the spring.

129. Which of the following three types of spring has self-damping properties? (*a*) **Coil spring.** (*b*) **Torsion-bar spring.** (*c*) **Laminated-leaf spring.**

The laminated-leaf spring.

130. What causes the self-damping action of the laminated-leaf spring?

The friction between the spring leaves.

131. What do the terms 'bump' and 'rebound' mean when applied to road springs or dampers?

Bump is when the spring or damper linkage is deflected upward, as when the wheel hits a bump.

Rebound is when the road wheel or damper linkage movement is downward, i.e. the opposite of bump.

Note: Bump and rebound are sometimes referred to as compression and extension respectively. Also, bump is sometimes called 'jounce.'

132. Dampers are sometimes classified as: *(a)* single-acting dampers, *(b)* double-acting dampers, or *(c)* double-acting differential dampers. Explain the meanings of these classifications.

(a) A single-acting damper (shock-absorber) is one that acts in one direction only, usually on rebound.

(b) A double-acting damper is one which acts on both bump and rebound.

(c) A double-acting differential damper is one which has a different damping effect on bump from rebound.

133. What is the basic operating principle of hydraulic dampers?

These dampers dissipate energy by forcing liquid under pressure through small holes or passages. This heats up the liquid and thus changes mechanical energy into heat energy. (The heat is dissipated to atmosphere through the body of the shock-absorber.)

134. Direct-acting (telescopic) dampers are very popular today. What are their advantages compared with the lever-arm (indirect-acting) type?

(a) Volume of fluid displaced is large, so that large amounts of energy can be dissipated without causing a high temperature rise.

(b) There are no trunnion bearings or connecting-arm pivots at which wear could develop.

(c) Fluid pressures are comparatively low, because of fairly large piston area and the absence of levers which increase the force applied to the damper, as found in the indirect types.

(d) Because of lower pressures and the fact that there is no rotating shaft entering the reservoir, leaks are much less likely.

(e) Generally cost is less.

(f) Many types do not require refilling to correct level during the life of the damper.

135. What routine maintenance do dampers require?

(a) If there is provision for refilling to correct level they should be refilled with the correct fluid at the recommended intervals.

(b) Mounting bolts and bushings should be checked.

136. What effects can weak dampers have on vehicle behavior?

(a) Ride is less comfortable due to continued flexing of the springs. *(b)* Vehicle is less stable since it may roll badly during cornering. *(c)* Vehicle will pitch heavily, particularly under hard braking.

LUBRICANTS AND OIL CONSUMPTION

137. Name three types of lubricant used on a vehicle.
(a) Oil. *(b)* Grease. *(c)* Graphite (carbon).

138. What special property has graphite as a lubricant and in what applications is it particularly useful?
Graphite is a dry lubricant. This property is particularly useful in such places as the release bearing of a dry clutch, the carbon brush in the distributor cap, and similar applications where the presence of oil or grease may be undesirable.

139. What is a lubricating oil additive?
A lubricating oil additive is any substance which is added to an oil in order to improve its performance. The additive may improve the natural properties of the lubricant, or confer on the oil properties that it would not otherwise possess.

140. Name some of the main functions of engine lubricating oil additives.
(a) To reduce oil oxidation due to high operating temperatures.
(b) To protect bearings from corrosion, caused by acidic products of combustion and lubricant decomposition.
(c) Detergency, i.e. keeping minute particles of contaminating matter in harmless suspension in the oil by preventing the particles from adhering to one another.
(d) To improve the viscosity index of an oil. This means that the oil will flow easily when cold and will not thin out excessively at engine-operating temperatures.
(e) To improve the 'oiliness' of an oil, thus enabling an oil film to cling more tenaciously to metal surfaces.
(f) Extreme-pressure additives are used to improve the load-carrying capacity of an oil.
(g) To reduce the foaming of oils, which may otherwise result in bearings receiving an inadequate supply of lubricant.
(h) To act as rust inhibitors. This is of particular importance when engines are run at low operating temperatures or are left standing outside for long periods.
(i) To prevent the formation of sludge.

141. Name five of the more important lubricating oil additives and say in what proportions might they be used.
(a) Viscosity index improvers, 2-10%.
(b) Anti-oxidants and corrosion inhibitors, 0.4-2%.

(c) Detergents, 2-10%.
(d) Oiliness agents, 0.1-1.0%.
(e) Extreme pressure agents, 5-10%.

142. What is meant by the 'viscosity' of an oil?
The viscosity of an oil is a measure of its ability to flow.

143. How is the viscosity of an oil measured?
It is the time in seconds that a measured quantity of oil takes to pass through an orifice of known size at a given temperature. (The figures vary according to the type of equipment used, and the temperature at which readings are taken.)

144. How are oils generally classified?
They are classified by their S.A.E. number, e.g. an engine oil may be classified as S.A.E. 20. Oils are given an appropriate S.A.E. number according to their viscosity at certain temperatures.

145. Is the S.A.E. rating of an oil an indication of anything else other than its viscosity?
No. An oil is placed in its particular S.A.E. class according to its viscosity rating only.

146. What is the 'viscosity index' of an oil?
This is a number which gives an indication of the rate of change of viscosity with change of temperature. If an oil is very 'thick' at low temperatures and very 'thin' at high temperatures, it would have a low viscosity index.

The less the change in viscosity with change in temperature, then the higher will be the viscosity index and (generally) the better the oil.

147. What is a 'multi-grade' oil?
It is an oil with a high viscosity index. That is to say, it is an oil which combines the desirable characteristics of a thin winter grade with the full-bodied properties of a summer grade.

148. What are three of the main differences between an engine oil and a rear axle oil?
(a) Rear axle oil is more viscous (thicker).
(b) Additives to combat contaminents due to combustion are not needed by rear axle oil.
(c) Due to very high tooth loadings that can occur, rear axle oil must contain a higher proportion of extreme pressure additives.

149. What is grease?
Grease is a mixture of about 80 per cent lubricating oil and a soap made from fatty acids and an alkali.

150. When is grease used in preference to oil?
(a) When the bearing would not easily retain oil.
(b) When low operating speeds and high pressures would break through or prevent the formation of an oil film.
(c) Where grit and water cannot be completely excluded.

151. Name three types of soap-bases used for grease.
(a) Lime base. (b) Sodium base. (c) Lithium.

152. What type of soap base do many multi-purpose greases employ and what are its advantages?
Lithium soap base. It has the advantage of being water-resistant and possessing a good buttery texture over a very wide temperature range.

153. How is the consistency of grease measured?
By dropping a metal cone of fixed weight and dimensions from a standard height on to the grease which is at a given temperature. The distance the cone sinks into the grease is recorded in tenths of a millimeter. The higher the figure, the softer the grease.

154. If an engine requires an excessive quantity of oil, yet the cylinder bores, pistons, and rings were in good order, what other possible causes could there be?
(a) Oil leaks. (b) Worn intake guides. (c) Wrong viscosity oil being used. (d) Oil pressure too high, causing leaks, or forcing more oil to be thrown on to the cylinder walls than could be satisfactorily dealt with by the piston rings. (e) Intake-valve stem seals worn or missing.

155. Should an engine consume oil?
Yes, a little. An engine in good condition, for example, will rarely need more than about 1 pint between oil changes. Some engines, however, particularly in the more expensive cars, are designed from the beginning to have a modest oil consumption.

VEHICLE STRUCTURE

156. Explain briefly what is meant by 'chassisless' or 'integral' construction.

This type of construction has no separate body and chassis. The entire structure is built up of light metal pressings secured together, usually by welding. In general all parts, including door pillars, windshield pillars, and roof, are load-carrying members. Suitable stiffening and strengthening sections are placed at points of maximum load, such as engine and suspension mountings. The only members not contributing to the stiffness of the structure are, normally, opening panels, such as the trunk and engine hood and the doors.

157. What are the advantages of integral construction over the conventional separate body and chassis arrangement?

(a) Reduced cost when manufactured in large numbers. (b) Lightness. (c) Greater torsional rigidity. (d) Improved vehicle performance and road-holding because of (b) and (c). (e) Less body rattle and squeaks. (f) On impact the body tends to crumple, thus absorbing some of the shock and reducing the effect of the impact on the passengers.

158. What are the disadvantages of integral construction?

(a) Only a small amount of corrosion can cause serious weakness to occur. (b) Production is only economic in very large quantities. (c) Resistance to impact damage is less. (d) Repair is often complicated and expensive. (e) This type of construction tends to amplify road and mechanical noises and very special care must be taken with sound insulation.

159. About how thick are the main body panels of a car of integral construction?

A typical thickness is 20 s.w.g. or 0.036 in.

160. What is a typical thickness of metal used for the structural members (such as door sills, windshield pillars, etc.) of a car of integral construction?

0.045 in.

161. Give four advantages of separate body and chassis construction?

(a) The body may not need to contribute to the overall strength of the vehicle. (b) Body style variations are easier and cheaper with this form of construction. (c) Generally, body repair work is easier and cheaper. (d) With commercial vehicles in particular individual types of body (e.g. 'one off') are quite practical propositions.

BRAZING AND WELDING

162. At what temperature are the following operations carried out? (a) Brazing. (b) Welding.

The temperatures in each of these operations vary according to the metals being used: (a) 700-950°C. (b) 1300°C (mild steel).

163. Give one typical example of where welding, brazing and soldering might be used on a motor vehicle.

(a) Welding a torn fender. (b) Brazing the flange on to an exhaust pipe. (c) Soldering a terminal on to a starter lead.

FAULT DIAGNOSIS

164. When attempting to diagnose the fault(s) of a vehicle, what should normally be the first stage of the procedure?

Ask the driver for his observations of the signs and symptoms.

165. Make a list of ten important parts of a vehicle that should be checked when inspecting a vehicle for roadworthiness.

(a) Brakes. (b) Steering. (c) Tires. (d) Lights. (e) Road springs. (f) Shock-absorbers. (g) Clutch. (h) Transmission. (i) Door catches. (j) Windshield-wipers.

166. What transmission defects may cause a vehicle to be regarded as unroadworthy?

(a) Difficulty in engaging or disengaging gears.

(b) Any tendency towards jumping out of gear.

167. Suggest three points that should be checked before checking 'toe-in.'

(a) Tire pressures. (b) Front-wheel bearings, king-pins, steering connections, and wheel nuts. (c) Wheels should not be out of true by more than 1/8 in.

168. Suggest four externally obvious tire defects that would make a vehicle unroadworthy?

(a) Side wall cuts. (b) Side walls bulging, ballooning or blistering. (c) Thread worn smoothe. (d) Tires of too small a section fitted.

169. When testing for satisfactory clutch operation, what checks should be made?

Check that the clutch does not slip or drag, and that engagement takes place smoothly without grab or chatter, and that there is sufficient free play at the pedal.

170. What would be a good braking efficiency for a hand-brake operating on two rear wheels only?

30 per cent.

171. What would be the minimum satisfactory foot-brake efficiencies for a car, a light commercial vehicle, and a public service vehicle?

There are no hard and fast values for this apart from Vehicle and Traffic Law State of N.Y. § 382 382 (a), but the following will be a good guide: (a) Car, 50 per cent. (b) Light commercial vehicles, 40 per cent. (c) Public-service vehicle, 30 per cent.

172. When an engine is using a fair amount of oil, how can one determine whether the oil is (a) being consumed by being burned within the cylinders, or (b) simply leaking away?

(a) By excessive blue exhaust smoke, particularly if the engine is revved after being allowed to idle for a few minutes. On removal, the spark plugs may show soft, oily, carbon deposits.

(b) Lack of the above symptoms. Leakage can be confirmed by placing a large, clean tray or sheet of paper under the engine and running the engine (at its normal operating temperature) at a speed equivalent to about 30 m.p.h. in top gear, for, say, 15 to 20 minutes. An odd tiny drop or two of oil can be ignored, but a larger amount in this time could indicate a leak worth investigating.

173. How much would a motor-car cylinder have to be worn before it required reboring?

There is no definite figure for this, but in the region of 0.006 in. to 0.010 in. and over.

174. State the purpose of each of the following items of garage equipment: (a) Exhaust-gas analyzer. (b) Cylinder-compression gauge. (c) Vacuum gauge. (d) Stroboscope.

(a) Checking the air/fuel ratio supplied by the carburetor. (b) Testing the compression pressure of an engine. (c) Mainly carburation and ignition timing setting. (d) This can be a flashing timing light used to check the ignition setting while the engine is running.

175. In most cases if the ignition is left switched on for an hour or more the coil burns out. In some cases, however, this does not occur. Why?

If, when the ignition is left on, the contact-breaker points are open, current cannot flow in the primary circuit. Consequently the coil cannot become overheated and burn out.

ENGINE NOISES

176. What are the symptoms of connecting rod bearing knock?

A fairly heavy, dull metallic knock evident when the engine is pulling under light load, and becoming more pronounced as the engine warms up and the oil thins out. Oil pressure gauge reading too low.

177. What are the symptoms of piston pin end knock?

A light, sharp metallic rattle, mainly audible if the engine is raced in neutral and the throttle quickly snapped shut. Some slight noise during idling.

178. What noise symptoms indicate a worn timing chain?

A 'thrashing' noise, most obvious when standing in front of the radiator when the engine is idling fairly slowly. The noise tends to disappear as the engine r.p.m. rises.

179. If one cylinder is knocking, how can it be traced?

Short out each plug in turn, and note which one causes the knock to disappear.

180. What sort of noise is caused by worn main bearings?

A heavy, low-pitched rumble, generally most audible when the engine is pulling hard in top gear.

181. What sort of noise is piston slap?

A fairly sharp metallic sound, at its worst with a cold engine and gradually diminishing as the engine warms up.

182. What sort of noise would indicate excessive tappet clearances?

A sharp, light, consistent clicking sound which alters in direct relation to the speed of the engine. Clearly audible at idling, especially with a cold engine.

CALCULATIONS, SCIENCE AND LABORATORY WORK

ABSOLUTE PRESSURE AND TEMPERATURE, AND GAS PROBLEMS

183. If an engine compression gauge showed a pressure of 130 PPSI, what would be the absolute pressure?

Absolute pressure = gauge pressure + atmospheric pressure
$$= 130 + 14.7$$
$$= 144.7 \text{ PPSI.}$$

184. If at the end of the compression stroke in a C.I. engine, the air was at a temperature of 600°C, what would be its absolute temperature, expressed in degrees Kelvin (°K)?

Absolute temperature °K = normal temperature (°C) + 273
$$= 600 + 273$$
$$= 873°\text{K.}$$

185. What is absolute zero Fahrenheit?
$-460°$F.

186. If a given mass of gas is kept at a constant temperature what, in simple terms, is the relationship between the volume and pressure of that gas?

If the volume decreases, the pressure rises; and if the volume increases the pressure falls. The relationship between pressure and volume being always in strict mathematical relationship.

187. What happens to a given volume of gas when its temperature is increased?

Its pressure rises in proportion to the rise in absolute temperature (°K).

188. What happens to a given mass of gas when its pressure remains constant, but the gas is heated?

The volume of the gas increases in proportion to its increase in absolute temperature.

189. What is the mathematical formula that expresses the relationship between the temperature, pressure, and volume of a gas, as dealt with in Questions 186, 187, and 188?

$$\frac{P_1 \cdot V_1}{T_1} = \frac{P_2 \cdot V_2}{T_2}$$

where P_1 = initial pressure
V_1 = initial volume
T_1 = Initial temperature (°K)
P_2 = final pressure
V_2 = final volume
T_2 = final temperature (°K)

Note: Pressure and temperature *must* be in absolute units.

ENGINE TESTING

190. What is a 'dynamometer' and for what purpose is it used?

A dynamometer is a machine used to absorb the power output of an engine and at the same time to measure the torque the engine is producing.

191. Name three types of dynamometers.

(a) Pony brake. (b) Electric. (c) Hydraulic, or water brake.

192. What is a 'tachometer'?

It is an instrument used to measure r.p.m. (often wrongly called a rev-counter).

193. When using a hydraulic dynamometer, what information would be needed to calculate engine torque at any given moment?

(a) The brake-load reading. (b) The length of the dynamometer arm. (c) R.P.M.

194. If an engine on test supported a brake load of 36 lbs and the length of the dynamometer arm was 14 in., what would be its torque output (a) in inch pounds, and (b) in ft pounds?

Torque = brake load × length of dynamometer arm

(a) Torque = 36 × 14 = 504 in. lbs.

(b) Torque = $\dfrac{36 \times 14}{12}$ = 42 ft lbs.

195. What is 'brake' horsepower?

B.h.p. is the amount of useful power developed by the engine and available to do useful work at the flywheel.

196. What is 'indicated' horsepower?

This is power actually developed in the cylinders. It is greater than the b.h.p. by the horsepower which is needed to overcome the pumping and friction losses of the engine (and to drive accessories such as water-pump and generator/alternator).

197. What is the 'friction' horsepower of an engine?

It is the difference between the i.h.p. and the b.h.p. of an engine, i.e. the horsepower required to overcome the pumping and friction losses of an engine.

Friction h.p. = i.h.p. − b.h.p.

198. Explain what is meant by the 'mechanical efficiency' of an engine, and say how it is usually expressed.

It is the ratio between the i.h.p. and the b.h.p. and is usually expressed as a percentage.

199. An engine develops 42 b.h.p. and 50 i.h.p. What will be its mechanical efficiency and the horsepower lost to friction?

$$\text{Mechanical efficiency} = \frac{\text{b.h.p.}}{\text{i.h.p.}} \times \frac{100}{1}$$

$$= \frac{42}{50} \times \frac{100}{1}$$

$$= 84\%$$

$$\text{Friction h.p.} = \text{i.h.p.} - \text{b.h.p.}$$

$$= 50 - 42$$

$$= 8 \text{ h.p.}$$

200. The usual formula to find the b.h.p. of an engine being dynamometer tested is: $\text{b.h.p.} = \dfrac{2\pi NT}{33,000}$. What easier formula is it sometimes possible to use?

$$\text{b.h.p.} = \frac{WN}{K},$$

where W = brake load in pounds
N = r.p.m.
K = constant for the particular dynamometer being used.

201. An engine on test at 5000 r.p.m. supports a brake load of 30 lb on an arm of 14-in. radius. The dynamometer constant K = 4500. Demonstrate that both the formulae mentioned in Question 200 will produce the same answer.

(a) $\text{b.h.p.} = \dfrac{2\pi NT}{33,000}$

$$= \frac{2 \times 22 \times 5000 \times 14 \times 30}{7 \times 33,000 \times 12}$$

$$= 33\text{-}1/3 \text{ h.p.}$$

(b) $\text{b.h.p.} = \dfrac{WN}{K}$

$$= \frac{30 \times 5000}{4500}$$

$$= 33\text{-}1/3 \text{ h.p.}$$

202. How is it possible to determine the i.h.p. of a multi-cylinder engine without the use of a cylinder pressure indicator?

By means of the Morse test.

203. Describe how to carry out a Morse test to ascertain the mechanical efficiency of a four-cylinder engine.

(a) Allow the engine to achieve its correct operating temperature. Run it at the desired r.p.m. and find the b.h.p. in the normal way with all the cylinders firing.

(b) To find the i.h.p., short out No. 1 cylinder and reduce the brake load to obtain the same r.p.m. used during the b.h.p. test. Note the brake-load reading. Then repeat this procedure for each cylinder.

(c) Calculate the b.h.p. with No. 1 cylinder cut out and subtract this from the b.h.p. all firing. The difference is the i.h.p. of No. 1 cylinder. Do this for each cylinder and add together the i.h.p.'s of every cylinder. The sum is the total i.h.p. of the engine.

(d) Calculate the mechanical efficiency as shown in the answer to Question 199.

204. During a Morse test on a four-cylinder engine, with all the cylinders firing, 40 b.h.p. was obtained. The b.h.p.'s obtained with each cylinder cut out in turn were, starting with No. 1, 28, 26.8, 29.2, and 27.5. Calculate the i.h.p. of the engine.

I.h.p. No. 1 cylinder = 40 − 28   = 12
I.h.p. No. 2 cylinder = 40 − 26.8 = 13.2
I.h.p. No. 3 cylinder = 40 − 29.2 = 10.8
I.h.p. No. 4 cylinder = 40 − 27.5 = 12.5

$$\text{Total i.h.p.} = 48.5$$

205. What formula is used to calculate the specific fuel consumption of an engine in pints per b.h.p. hour?

$$\text{Pints per b.h.p. hour} = \frac{\text{pints of fuel used per hour}}{\text{b.h.p.}}$$

206. An engine produces 15 b.h.p. and consumes 0.25 pints of fuel in 125 sec. What is its specific fuel consumption in pints per b.h.p. hour?

$$\text{Pints per b.h.p. hour} = \frac{\text{pints of fuel used per hour}}{\text{b.h.p.}}$$

$$= \frac{0.25 \times 60 \times 60}{125 \times 15}$$

$$= 0.48 \text{ pints per b.h.p. hour}$$

207. An engine develops a torque of 60 ft lbs at 3000 r.p.m. and drives through a transmission with second gear of 3:1 ratio engaged. With a final drive reduction of 5:1, at what speed with the axle-shafts rotate, and if the transmission efficiency is 85 per cent, what will be the torque applied to the axle-shafts?

$$\text{Axle-shaft r.p.m.} = \frac{\text{engine r.p.m.}}{\text{overall gear ratio}}$$

$$= \frac{3000}{3 \times 5}$$

$$= 200 \text{ r.p.m.}$$

$$\text{Torque on axle-shafts} = \text{engine torque} \times \text{overall gear ratio} \times \text{efficiency}$$

$$= 60 \times 3 \times 5 \times \frac{85}{100}$$

$$= 765 \text{ ft lbs.}$$

ELECTRICAL

HEAVY-DUTY STARTER MOTORS

208. What is a pre-engaged starter?

A starter-motor which has its pinion pushed into mesh with the ring-gear before the full starting current is switched on.

209. What is an 'axial,' or 'co-axial' starter?

These also are starter-motors whose pinions mesh with the ring-gear teeth before the full starting current is switched on.

210. To what type of engines are the starters, mentioned in the previous two questions, usually fitted?

To large C.I. engines and sometimes to gasoline engines intended for cold climates.

211. By what means is a heavy duty starter-motor often protected from overloading?

The drive from the motor to the pinion is transmitted via a small multi-plate clutch. The clutch is designed to slip if the load on the starter is too great.

212. On heavy duty C.I. engine starters the pinion drive is so arranged that the pinion cannot be thrown out of mesh from the ring-gear, until the starter-button is released. Why is this?

When starting from very cold, such an engine may make a number of isolated firing strokes which would throw an inertia-drive pinion out of mesh and yet not start the engine. The positive engagement of the pinion ensures that the starter remains in mesh and can continue to rotate the engine until it is able to run under its own power.

D.C. GENERATOR/ALTERNATOR

213. On what basic principle does the generator/alternator depend for current generation?
The passing of a conductor through a magnetic field — this induces a current in the conductor.

214. Upon what three things does generator/alternator output depend?
(a) The strength of the magnetic field. (b) The number of armatures (i.e. armature windings). (c) Armature r.p.m.

215. How is generator output controlled on a motor vehicle?
By varying the strength of the magnetic field.

216. What is the name of the equipment used to vary automatically the strength of a generator's magnetic field and what is their common operating principle?
(a) On older cars, a compensated voltage regulator.
(b) On newer models, a current-voltage regulator.
Both systems use the principle of increasing or decreasing the resistance of the generator field circuit to reduce or increase the generator output. This is effected by an automatic vibrating switch in parallel with a field resistance. The longer the periods during which the switch is closed (by-passing the resistance), the higher will be the generator output, and vice versa.

217. With their covers removed, how may a compensated voltage control unit be easily distinguished from a current-voltage control unit?
The compensated voltage unit has two coils, while the current-voltage unit has three coils.

218. What are the first simple, yet important, checks to make if a generator is not charging?
(a) Make sure that fan-belt is not slipping.
(b) Make a visual inspection for broken leads, loose terminals, blown field fuse, and the like.

219. How may the 'residual field' of a generator by checked?
(a) Disconnect generator leads. (b) Connect voltmeter between
"A" terminal on generator and ground. (c) With engine at approximately 1500 r.p.m., voltmeter should read 1.5 to 3.0V.

220. Describe briefly how to check generator field coils.
(a) Leave voltmeter in position described in (b) of previous test.
(b) Connect ammeter between "A" and "F" on generator.
(c) Gradually increase engine speed until nominal battery voltage
is registered on voltmeter (i.e. 6V or 12V). Ammeter should then
read approximately 2 Amps.

221. How can the voltage regulator setting be checked?
(a) Generator cables must be replaced after previous tests as in
Questions 219 and 220.
(b) Remove battery leads from control box, i.e. 'A' and 'A1' Compensated Voltage Regulator, or 'B' Current-Voltage Regulator.
(c) If two, or more, leads have been disconnected join them
together.
(d) Connect voltmeter between 'A' on regulator and ground.
(e) Run generator at charging speed and check that voltage is
within the manufacturer's recommended limits.

**222. What are the 'manufacturer's recommended limits' for volt-
age regulator settings, mentioned in the previous question?**
These vary according to the type of generator used, its control
equipment, and the temperature during the test.
Typical examples are (at 68°F):
Compensated Voltage system 16.0 - 16.6V.
Current-voltage system 14.9 - 15.5V.

**223. In what way can the current regulator be checked (current-
voltage control units only)?**
(a) Short out contacts of voltage regulator by means of a jumper
lead.
(b) Disconnect lead from 'B' terminal and insert ammeter in
series.
(c) Run generator at charging speed.
(d) Ammeter readings should be checked against specification.
(Note: This varies widely according to type of generator.)

224. What is the function of a cut-out and where is it located?
(a) It prevents the battery from discharging via the generator,
when the generator voltage falls below battery voltage.
(b) It is located in series between the battery and generator.

225. What is the cutting-in voltage of a cut-out?

The voltage when the cut-out points close to allow current to flow from the generator to the battery. It should be between 12.7-13.3V.

226. What is the function of the ignition or (more properly) the generator warning light?

(a) It serves as a reminder that the driver had left the ignition switched on.

(b) When it goes out as the engine r.p.m. rises, it indicates that the generator is charging.

227. How is the generator warning light connected in the car's electrical system?

The light is connected from the coil side of the ignition switch to the insulated main generator brush, via the "A" terminal on the regulator.

228. How does the generator warning light work?

With the ignition switched on and the generator stopped (or rotating slowly), battery current flows through the lamp and is grounded through the generator. As the generator current rises, it opposes the flow of battery current through the lamp and the lamp goes out. (The main charging current goes to the battery through the cut-out.)

A. C. GENERATOR

229. What item of normal electrical equipment does an a.c. generator (or alternator) replace?

The normal generator.

230. What advantages does an alternator possess over a conventional generator?

(a) Higher maximum output. *(b)* Increased low speed output. *(c)* More robust, but lighter. *(d)* Virtually no maintenance necessary. *(e)* Can be operated at higher r.p.m. without damage. *(f)* A separate cut-out is not required. *(g)* Regulation system is simpler. *(h)* Output current does not go through brushes.

231. Why is a separate cut-out not needed with an alternator?

The output is rectified by means of semi-conductor diodes and since these can only conduct current one way, reverse flow from battery to alternator is impossible.

232. What are three essential precautions to observe when working on cars fitted with alternators, but not fitted with generators?

(a) Do not connect the battery leads to the wrong battery terminals, even for an instant.

(b) Remove battery ground cable if battery is to receive a rapid charge.

(c) Remove battery ground cable if electric welding is to be done on the car.

233. Compare the principal features of an alternator (a.c. generator) and a generator.

Alternator

(a) Magnetic field produced by rotor.

(b) Power generated in stator.

(c) Output rectified by semiconductor diodes.

Generator

(a) Magnetic field produced by field coils (stator).

(b) Power generated in rotor (i.e. armature).

(c) Output rectified by commutator.